Arming the British Police

Also by Roy Ingleton:

Police of the World
Police Vehicles of the World
*Mission Incomprehensible – The Linguistic Barrier to Policing
    Europe*
Elsevier's French/Engish Dictionary of Police & Criminal Law
The Gentlemen at War – Policing Britain 1939–45
European Strategic Alliances (translation)

ARMING THE BRITISH POLICE
The Great Debate

Roy Ingleton

*Those entrusted with arms ... should be persons
of some substance and stake in the country*

William Windham (1750–1810)
House of Commons, 22 July 1807

FRANK CASS
LONDON • PORTLAND, OR

Published in 1997 in Great Britain by
FRANK CASS & CO. LTD.
Newbury House, 900 Eastern Avenue,
London IG2 7HH, England

and in the United States of America by
FRANK CASS
c/o ISBS, 5804 N.E. Hassalo Street
Portland, Oregon, 98213-3644

British Library Cataloguing in Publication Data:

A catalogue record for this book is available
from the British Library

ISBN 0-7146-4741-1 (cloth)
ISBN 0-7146-4299-1 (paperback)

Library of Congress Cataloging-in-Publication Data:

A catalog record for this book is available
from the Library of Congress

363.23/

Printed in Great Britain by
Bookcraft (Bath) Ltd, Midsomer Norton, Avon

Contents

List of Tables

Introduction

Newspaper headlines, television and radio news broadcasts and public opinion, all speak of the violent society which exists in Great Britain in these, the final years of the twentieth century. Many honest citizens despair at the apparent impossibility of curbing the ever-growing number of robberies, burglaries, muggings and even murder. Indeed, so widespread is the fear of violent crime that there are frequent, strident calls for our traditionally unarmed policemen and women to be issued with guns and to carry firearms routinely, whenever they are on duty.

Even the police themselves, for many years totally opposed to the idea of being armed, are more and more coming round to the view that the day is fast approaching when this state of affairs will arise.

Despite the undoubted high levels of serious crime which we are experiencing, there remains an equally vehement and convinced body of opinion which sees the arming of the police as the last straw, the 'end of civilization as we know it'. It is maintained that the police in the United Kingdom (excepting, of course, Northern Ireland during the terrorist activities there) have always been unarmed and any change in this policy is viewed by many with dismay.

But is this entirely true? Many readers will be surprised at the extent to which the police have carried firearms in the past and even the present-day proliferation of armed police officers is not always appreciated. Certainly there are cogent arguments both for and against a routinely armed police service and the aim of this book is to take a cool and dispassionate look at the position, to weigh up the perceived advantages and disadvantages of this undoubtedly grave step and to try to provide a sound platform on which to base any ultimate decision.

How do they manage in other countries? Many police officers throughout the world – perhaps the majority – carry a firearm whenever they are on duty, but although Britain is unusual in having an unarmed police service it is by no means alone. The decision whether or not to arm the police tends to be based on the national temperament as well as on historical and traditional grounds. It is often asserted that the phlegmatic British are less volatile than the populace in other countries, but is this assumption based on fact? And has the British character changed so much over recent years that an armed police force is now necessary? What in fact is the experience of those countries which have long been accustomed to seeing a policeman with a pistol on his hip, or more discreetly concealed beneath his jacket or under his armpit? The example of the United States is often cited, especially by the opponents of the proposal, but is this a valid comparison? Should we not look closer to home and examine the police forces in Europe and in the former British Dominions in Canada and the Antipodes?

Bearing all these factors in mind, this book examines the history of violent crime in the United Kingdom and the extent to which this has been directed towards the police themselves in order to determine whether the police are now facing, as is often believed, a greater danger than ever before.

The issuing of firearms and other weapons to the police over the years and the more recent introduction of armed response vehicles is also examined, as are a limited number of occasions when actual use has been made of such weapons. The usual arguments for and against the issuing of firearms to the police will be aired and viewed in the light of the experience gained in a number of other countries in Europe, as well as in the USA, Australia and New Zealand. How often do the police in these countries resort to the use of firearms and under what circumstance? Does the carrying and use of firearms by the police provoke an increased use of firearms by the criminal element and a higher level of serious assaults on the guardians of law and order?

The object of this review is to cut away some of the hysterical overreaction surrounding this emotive issue and to try to provide reasoned arguments which may be taken into account by those who wish to make their voices heard, as well as by those who will have to make the ultimate and fateful decision.

1 Aux armes, citoyens!

> No civilized nation ... has to lament, as we have, the daily commission of the most dangerous and atrocious crimes, in so much that we cannot travel the roads, or sleep in our houses ... without the most imminent danger of thieves and robbers ...

A sentiment which will be echoed by many readers, alarmed at the current levels of crime in Great Britain. But, in fact, this was written over 200 years ago.[1] So are things really so much worse than they were at the end of the eighteenth century, when there was no real police force as we know it?

A contemporary writer suggests that they are not:

> Take crime. We are living in a period where law-breaking seems to be rising inexorably. But history shows that crime moved in long waves, rising and falling for a complex variety of reasons. On a long historical view, levels are quite low – compared to the eighteenth or early nineteenth century. They are merely high compared with the fifties, a very unusual period.[2]

So this earlier period might be a good point at which to start our survey of violent crime in England and Wales.

The end of the eighteenth century was certainly a period of great unrest; there were revolutions in France and elsewhere and a bitterly fought War of Independence conducted in our American colonies. Although spared the Terror of revolutionary France and the turmoil elsewhere in Europe, the citizens of England, or at least the middle and upper classes, were

1

apprehensive of a popular uprising matching those occurring on the continent. Already, in 1780, there had been serious rioting in protest against the Catholic Relief Act when Lord George Gordon led a crowd in a march on Parliament to present a petition. The ensuing disorder lasted a week, during which time a great deal of damage was done and, for a time, London was taken over by the mob. The Army was mobilized and, in suppressing the riots, some 200 protesters were shot dead by the military.

As the years went by, further riots occurred as a result of food shortages and rising prices and the recruiting demands associated with the Napoleonic Wars. With the country in the throes of the Industrial Revolution, a displaced and disenfranchized rural population was being compelled for economic reasons to make drastic changes in its lifestyle and to adjust to different work disciplines, all accompanied by unaccustomed pressures on family life. Between 1811 and 1815 these pressures and frustrations culminated in demonstrations against the mechanization of the weaving trade in the East Midlands, Lancashire and Yorkshire. Inspired by Ned Ludd, rioters destroyed the machinery which they saw as destroying their livelihood and the mill owners again called for the deployment of troops (there was still no regular police force in the country). So far-reaching were these events that the term 'Luddites' has now passed into the English language to describe those who are violently resistant to change and progress.

But perhaps the climax came in 1819 when a crowd of around 60,000 gathered in St Peter's Fields in Manchester to listen to speakers demanding the repeal of the highly unpopular Corn Laws. Fearing that the inflammatory speeches would lead to disorder, the magistrates ordered the mounted Yeomanry to charge the crowd to disperse it. The repeated charges resulted in 11 people losing their lives while over 400 were injured. Coming so soon after the great victory of Waterloo, the event was quickly satirized as the 'Battle of Peterloo'.

However, serious as public disorder is, it is not the only form of illegal violence and most people think of murder, robbery, rape and offences of that nature as 'violent crime', rather than riot, affray or unlawful assembly, which are frequently regarded as political rather than criminal. Certainly the average citizen has more to fear from the robber or burglar, whom he cannot always avoid, than from riotous demonstrators, with whom he usually need not get involved.

The problem in seeking to establish crime levels in Georgian England is the total lack of statistics before 1805. However, based on such evidence as exists (court records and newspaper reports, for instance) one historian suggests that there appeared to be a gradual increase in theft and assaults in the last half of the eighteenth century, becoming much steeper in the first quarter of the nineteenth.[3] This evolution may be attributed to increases in the population, a growing urbanism and capitalization of industry, and a general increase in personal possessions. There was, in fact, more to steal!

Even at the beginning of the period under review, there were complaints that:

> I sup with my friend; I cannot return to my home, not even in my chariot, without danger of a pistol being clapt to my breast. I build an elegant villa, ten or twenty miles distant from the capital: I am obliged to provide an armed force to convey me thither, lest I should be attacked on the road with fire and ball.[4]

Around the same time, the conclusion of the American War of Independence led George III to express his concern that 'the number of persons this peace will occasion' would increase the number of highwaymen. It is true that foreign wars tended to remove from these shores the active young men who might otherwise become involved in some form of crime. In fact, in time of war, those who committed crimes were often given the option of 'volunteering' for the Army as an alternative to transportation. But the country was experiencing a demographic explosion hitherto undreamed of. Throughout the first half of the eighteenth century the population of England and Wales remained fairly static at around six million – fewer than the present population of London alone – but it then started to increase and to increase rapidly. In the 20 years up to 1770 the population of London doubled and, nation-wide, the figure had reached 18 million by 1851. This meant that the average age was falling fast and the labour market was saturated with young persons, not all of whom could be found jobs, and it is the young who are traditionally the main authors of crimes and acts of violence.

The sharp increase in crime following the Napoleonic Wars is well documented (although perhaps inadequately explained) and resulted in a flurry of legislation aimed at rogues and vagabonds, idle and disorderly persons, beggars and those wandering abroad without visible means of support. The belief that crime was rising out of control was one of the great social factors affecting life in Georgian England and helped to formulate these Draconian laws and punishments. Despite the perception of the Middle Ages as a period of great cruelty, it is interesting to note that in the century and a half following the crowning of Charles II in 1660, 187 new capital statutes became law – nearly six times as many as in the preceding 300 years. One Act alone prescribed the death penalty for over 200 offences, most of which were aimed at the protection of property rather than persons; attempted murder was merely a misdemeanour until 1803. Homicide was not, in fact, a statistically prominent offence. It was a general anxiety about murder and robbery with violence – the 'fear of crime' – which led to more stringent legislation in 1752; but there were only ten convictions for murder that year, and that was exceptionally high for the times. The annual average murder rate in London and Middlesex between 1750 and 1770 was just four. Elsewhere, murder as a corollary of robbery was extremely rare and most homicides were of a 'domestic' nature.

This broad-brush approach to crime and punishment makes any comparison with modern times much more difficult. On the one hand, in the second half of the eighteenth century there were 3,608 capital convictions in London and Middlesex alone, resulting in 1,650 executions; but these represented a wide variety of comparatively minor crimes. On the other hand, the fact that conviction would inexorably result in the death penalty undoubtedly swayed a number of juries in the delivery of their verdict. In fact, crime continued to rise despite these measures until at least the middle of the nineteenth century.

One of the problems in the period up until the second quarter of the nineteenth century was the lack of an effective police system. Although France had long had its laws enforced by a police force in Paris and a *maréchaussée* in the countryside, these were regarded as totally foreign and abhorrent to any decent-thinking Englishman; the idea was not compatible with his concept of liberty! England continued to rely largely on parish constables (often merely part-time) in the countryside and a system of watchmen in the towns and cities. Many of the latter, known as 'Charlies', were elderly, often infirm and of little use against determined young thieves. Although usually armed with a cutlass, they tended to avoid any kind of confrontation by rapping their staff on the pavement as they walked their beat to give any criminals a timely warning of their approach. Failing this, they were easily bribed and were thus of minimal value as a crime prevention measure. Much more reliance was placed by the magistrates on the system of rewards which prompted a number of active men, not always of unimpeachable character themselves, to act as thief-takers, following the example of the famous Jonathan Wild (1683–1725).

Most orthodox historians accept the arguments put forward by the nineteenth-century police reformers: first, that the old parochial system of policing was, at best, inefficient, and secondly, that England at the end of the eighteenth and the beginning of the nineteenth century was facing a serious increase in crime and disorder:

> ... there is no exaggeration in saying that, at the dawn of the nineteenth century, England was passing through an epoch of criminality darker than at any other in her annals.[5]

But, as has already been pointed out, it is extremely difficult to measure any increase in the levels of crime and disorder even in a society which keeps reliable statistics, and there were none at all kept in eighteenth-century England. There is a degree of agreement between historians, based on court records, that at this time larceny was probably increasing. The statistics kept from 1805 show a steady increase continuing until the middle of the nineteenth century. But how much of the recorded increase was due to an actual increase in occurrences of theft and how many could be put down to better policing, encouraging the reporting of crimes?

Where serious crimes of violence occurred these were the subject of public concern and outcry. It was the brutal murder of two East London families in December 1811 and known as the Ratcliffe Highway murders that led to the setting up of the first of four Parliamentary Select Committees on the policing of the capital. Resistance to any form of centrally organized police force continued to be expressed by both the public and many Parliamentarians. The working class saw, with some justification, the existence of an organized police force as a means of further repressing the poorer and disenfranchized members of the community, while the landowning class objected to having to fund a force which was to them unnecessary since they could protect themselves and their property quite adequately using their stewards, gamekeepers and other paid servants. Only the burgeoning middle class, the shopkeepers, mill owners and other small businessmen, saw any advantage in the proposals. Even when serious disorder in Lancashire led Sir Robert Peel to contemplate a reform of the policing of rural areas, public hostility to the idea of a police force controlled from Westminster remained firm; the proposals still smacked too much of the despised French system. That is not to say that there was not concern about the levels of crime and disorder outside London; towards the end of the 1820s the citizens of Cheshire were expressing their concern at the 'wide-spreading and awfully increasing dissemination of crime'.[6]

By this time a limited number of criminal statistics were available, having been introduced in 1805 and revised in 1834 to show crimes under six main headings:

1 Offences against the person;
2 Theft involving violence (including burglary);
3 Offences of theft not involving violence;
4 Offences against property (malicious damage);
5 Currency and coinage offences;
6 Miscellaneous offences.

Statistics are notoriously unreliable and these were certainly no exception. The existence of a dark figure (crimes committed but not reported) was known even at the end of the eighteenth century with Patrick Colquhoun noting that: 'there is not above one offence in one hundred that is discovered or prosecuted',[7] while nearly 40 years later, Edwin Chadwick found that: 'the number of cases pursued bore little or no relation to the cases of crime actually committed. We found large masses of crime with scarcely any pursuit at all.'[8]

But these comments refer to all types of crime. What about serious crime? What about murder and robbery with violence? In the decade between 1805 and 1815 there were around 15 convictions for murder each year (of whom some 13 were executed). In addition, around 35 were convicted of highway robbery each year in the same period, only around ten per cent of whom were executed. With a total population of about 12 million, these represent a murder ratio of 1:800,000 and a robbery ratio of 1:343,000. If one multiplies these figures by 4.25 to reflect the 1991 population of England and Wales, the number of murders would total 64 and robberies around 150. In fact, in 1991 there were around 200 convictions for murder and 5,100 for robbery. Can a threefold increase in the murder rate be entirely attributed to better reporting records or an improved detection rate? Almost certainly not. And no amount of statistical juggling can explain away a thirtyfold increase in robberies.

Meanwhile, the political and economic situation which afflicted the country sparked off a great many violent demonstrations in the period following Waterloo and which continued for some 30 years. The New Poor Law and the proposed electoral reform were widely unpopular and were the subject of several large-scale demonstrations, while the Chartist movement provoked other disorders. The late 1830s and 1840s saw a serious economic depression, giving rise to the term 'The Hungry Forties' and so, although Great Britain managed to escape the revolutions which characterized many European states in 1830 and 1848, the country was nevertheless wracked with internal disorder. The term *les classes dangereuses*, used by H. A. Frégier to describe the militant citizens of Paris, was quickly coined by the bourgeoisie in this country, although it has to be said that the British urban poor were much less of a danger than their French counterparts. Nevertheless, there was a riot of starving field hands in 1830, as a result of which three were hanged and 400 transported.

This civil unrest which, coupled with the growing crime figures, to a large extent prompted the formation of the Metropolitan Police in 1829, did not disappear with the formation of the force, much to the chagrin of the proponents of the New Police system. The Metropolitan Police was, of course, formed to police the metropolis of London and it is much to the credit of these pioneers that disorder in the capital was minimal, or at least much lower than in some provincial cities and in the countryside. Such was the rapidly growing reputation of this new panacea for all society's ills that the Metropolitan Police were frequently called upon to assist in quelling violent disorders in other areas.

The introduction of a properly organized police in London was quickly copied by a number of other cities, although on the whole the counties were slower to recognize the need for policing on a similar style. The formation of these police forces had, paradoxically, an unfortunate effect on the crime statistics. Certainly many more criminal offences were reported but it is not clear to what extent this was a reflection of increasing crime levels or whether the existence of organized police forces, with proper police stations and the opportunity for the poor to get someone to deal with their problems when they fell victims to crime, merely led to hitherto unreported crimes receiving proper attention. The number of committals to courts of Quarter Sessions and Assizes increased sevenfold in the years 1805 to 1842, to reach a peak of 31,309 in that latter year. There are indications that crime rose steadily during the first half of the nineteenth century, to level out or decline in the second.

Although a great deal of crime was committed in the poorer urban areas, this was by no means the whole picture. It was not uncommon for rural labourers to gang up on anyone passing through the field in which they were harvesting and demand money. Others went from door to door asking for money, their numbers and demeanour being such that few dared refuse. Lord Fortescue spoke of the situation in Devonshire whereby 'sturdy beggars, particularly in summer, invade our farmhouses and cottages and, in the absence of the men, extort money or provisions from the women whom they find at home'. The country towns, too, were not immune and many were plagued with gangs of young men who specialised in aggressive harassment, poaching and robbery.

The latter half of the nineteenth century was much more peaceful, although William Murray, the anti-Catholic agitator, provoked no fewer than 25 separate riots between 1866 and 1871. Once these started the police were quite unable to stop the disorders, even with help from the Special Constabulary, the Yeomanry and the Militia. In Birmingham, in 1867, 40 borough constables, 180 men from the county constabulary, 93 cavalry, 300 infantrymen and 500 special constables failed to contain the violence which resulted from one of his meetings.

In 1884 there were reports of baton and cavalry charges against demonstrating Fabians in Trafalgar

Square, while on 'Bloody Sunday' in 1887, three demonstrators were killed and over 200 injured at another Fabian meeting, during which the unemployed camped out in the Square.

Apart from politically inspired disorders, there were also some specific areas such as the Irish quarters in York and Wolverhampton, for example, which were particularly prone to rioting in the 30 or 40 years following the great potato famine, and some of these districts became virtual no-go areas for the local police. A similar area was the St. Giles 'rookery' in London which, from at least 1750 until it was demolished to make way for the cutting of New Oxford Street, was a hot-bed of crime and one in which any criminal fleeing the forces of law and order could be assured of a cordial welcome and active assistance in avoiding arrest.

At the same time, significant crime trends may be distinguished. To begin with there were the spates of garrottings in London in the mid-1850s and in 1862. Although there were only 15 recorded cases of robbery with violence in the whole of the Metropolitan Police District in the first six months of 1862, such was the fear generated by this version of the crime that the number of reports of garrottings rose to 46 in the last three months of the year alone. Was this due to a widespread increase in this type of crime, or was it simply a case of the increased publicity prompting more of the 'grey figures' being reported? There is also no doubt that some ordinary cases of robbery with violence or accompanied by menaces, were described as garrotting so as to be more 'fashionable'.

Certainly, the years which followed saw an unprecedented increase in robberies with violence and by 1866 there were 217 cases reported, resulting in 136 arrests – a commendable 'clear-up rate' by any standards.

A cursory glance at the crime statistics around this

time might lead one to assume that the level of serious crime generally was diminishing (and some politicians were quick to make such a claim), but the true reason lies in the fact that a number of misdemeanours were made non-indictable and thus did not figure in the statistics. Nevertheless, although industrialization and urbanization initially inspired crime and disorder, the disciplines inherent in urban life soon reversed this trend so that there was a definite fall in crime and disorder from 1860 to 1920. Clive Emsley[9] supports the hypothesis that there was a gradual decline in theft and crimes of violence during the second half of the nineteenth century, although burglary and housebreaking noticeably increased. There were, however, marked peaks and troughs in all these crimes and misdemeanours.

So far as homicide was concerned, this peaked at a ratio of two per 100,000 in 1865 and settled at around 1.5 per 100,000 for the rest of the century, declining still further as the new century dawned. With a population of 20 million, and despite the efforts of Jack the Ripper in 1889, there were rarely more than 40 homicides in any year between 1857 and 1890, falling still further to under 35 in the 1890s and most of these were 'domestic'. Cases of malicious wounding followed a similar pattern.

Despite the grinding poverty suffered by a great many in Victorian England, it seems that drink was the prime motivation for crime, rather than acquisitiveness or greed. In fact the 'demon drink' was even seen as a mitigating circumstance, as in the case reported in *The Times* on 16 March 1850 in which three men were charged at York with the murder of Mary Duggan, 'a woman of abandoned character'. One night she was seen to leave a public house with the three accused men and apparently went to a field where her body was discovered the next day 'with her person exposed and much bruised'. The judge directed the jury to acquit the defendants saying, 'these facts do not amount to manslaughter. The woman, being intoxicated, had voluntarily accompanied the prisoners; and she was not like an infant who, unable to take care of itself, had been left exposed to the cold and died in consequence'.

It is possible that drink was a factor in the spate of 'Cornerman' attacks which occurred in Liverpool around 1875. Unemployed, casual, dock labourers would hang around street corners and accost any strangers, asking for money. A refusal would be met with violence and at least one visitor to the area died as a result of his injuries. It is significant that these robbers were invariably supported by the locals against the police.

Mass violence in the twentieth century was usually associated with unemployment. Following the pattern set by the post-Napoleonic Wars period, in 1919 there were serious riots in Wolverhampton, Salisbury, Epsom, Luton, Essex, Coventry, Swindon and many parts of London, involving demobilized servicemen who were unable to find work in this 'land fit for heroes to live in' which they had been promised. These riots were mirrored during the next two years when unemployed demonstrators were involved in running battles with the police in Sheffield, Bristol, Birmingham, London, Liverpool, Leicester, Cardiff, Dundee and Glasgow. A decade later the Depression had hit the country and prompted even more riots, resulting in more than 100 baton charges in the period from August 1931 to December 1932.

All this time, the pattern of other forms of violent crime remained largely unchanged and fairly low-key. Homicides continued to be largely family affairs while robberies were usually committed with the aid of coshes and bludgeons and rarely involved the use of firearms. Burglaries were largely clandestine affairs, carried out in the absence of the occupants or, where the premises were occupied, by employing a high degree of stealth in order to avoid confrontation.

The outbreak of war in 1939 brought mass unemployment to an end and marked a change in crime patterns. That year there were 300,000 indictable offences recorded but the numbers fell markedly in the first months of the war, only to rise significantly throughout the war years, to peak at 478,000 in 1945. Most of the increase was for theft of one form or another, crimes of violence increasing but little. Convictions for homicide (murder and manslaughter) remained steady at just under 100 per annum, of which around 25 were classified as murder. The number of homicides rose to 122 in 1945, possibly due to a combination of returning ex-servicemen and unfaithful wives. On average there were 128 murders discovered in each of the war years which, given the number of convictions which has just been alluded to and allowing for multiple murders, indicates that the detection rate was little more than 20 per cent.[10]

The tendency for the 'peace-loving' Englishman to take to the streets in violent protest in emulation of his more volatile European cousins continued with but a brief respite during the post-war years. The crushing poverty of eighteenth- and nineteenth-century Britain was no longer a cause for unrest and demonstrations were now of a manifestly political nature, usually inspired by extreme activists from both sides of the political coin, or of a racial nature.

The streets were largely peaceful for the first three decades after the Second World War and the more recent manifestations of public dissatisfaction began with a riot in Red Lion Square in June 1974 when a provocative rally called by the National Front was attacked by supporters of the International Marxist Group. In the violence which followed one demonstrator lost his life and several people were injured, including police officers. The National Front were again involved in disorders in Lewisham in August 1977 when a march organized by them was the subject of indignant retaliation by (mainly) Asian and black residents, and in Southall two years later when, once again, a demonstrator was killed.

The comparative peace of post-war Britain having been broken, disturbances continued into the early 1980s with riots in Brixton and Southall which quickly spread to several other cities such as Liverpool, Manchester and Bristol. Other, sporadic disorders followed but the country enjoyed a period of relative calm from the middle of the 1980s.

Crime, however, did not take a holiday and, in fact, escalated alarmingly from around the 1960s. Undoubtedly a lot of this was directly related to illegal drug trafficking while a general relaxing of moral standards, induced by the permissive 1960s played no small part. However, it is not the purpose of this work to analyse the causes of crime; merely to comment on the trends as they are observed. Thus the latter half of the 1980s was characterized by the phenomenon of 'steaming' in which large numbers of youths, both black and white, used their numbers and the anonymity afforded by the gang to rob passengers on underground trains or to strip shops of their wares. The numbers involved (up to 200) and the fact that many were clearly armed with knives and other weapons rendered them free from interference.

The Conservative government elected in 1979 both promised and planned to control crime and disorder. In the event, crime rose to heights unprecedented since records were first kept nearly two centuries earlier, while riots and disorders were the worst in living memory. The menace of the drug dealers in modern times has provided yet a further burden for an already

15

hard-pressed police service. In 1994 one undercover detective dealing with serious crimes in the Manchester area faced prosecution arising out of an allegation that he illegally kept a gun for his personal protection. Having been subjected to death threats by Moss Side drug dealers, the officer's fears for his safety, and that of his family were such that he suffered a nervous breakdown.

This survey of violent crime and disorder over the past two centuries clearly demonstrates that, while unruly demonstrations have continued at sporadic intervals over the years, there is little to show that the violence has increased or worsened. Eleven rioters were killed at Peterloo in 1819 and a few of their descendants have been killed and injured in more recent times. As the numbers involved in the riots have undoubtedly increased with the growth in population and increasing urbanization, the decrease in serious injuries and deaths is probably due more to the improved methods of crowd control rather than any decrease in the level of violence. No longer do the military bear down on rioters with cutlasses drawn and pistols at the ready; truncheons and riot shields – even tear gas and baton rounds, although undoubtedly painful – are seldom life-threatening.

Crime, however, including violent crime, has undergone a considerable increase, as has the use of firearms. Excluding murders and assaults, in the first six months of 1991 there were 1,431 indictable offences committed in the Metropolitan Police District in which firearms were involved. The vast majority of these (1,329) were armed robberies and the main targets for these robberies were, somewhat surprisingly, shops and stalls (25 per cent) while banks and building societies came a close second. However, although firearms were often brandished, the number of occasions when shots were fired was comparatively small and, in fact, there were indications that, quite often, the weapons involved were either replicas or incapable of being fired.

Nevertheless:

> Every day in London an armed criminal fires one or two shots, either during a robbery, while enforcing territory for drug dealing, at the police or at another villain. Innocent members of the public are being put at risk.[11]

Elderly women, girls and old men are no longer immune from attack – far from it. They are often apparently seen as an easy touch. But what about the policeman and policewoman? Are they, too, the targets for violent assaults? In the next chapter we look at how the public – in particular that growing proportion which has little respect for the law – has over the years vented its spleen and relieved its frustrations on that guardian of law and order – the constable.

2 The policeman's lot

In the late eighteenth and the early nineteenth century preventive policing was largely confined to the growing urban areas where watchmen patrolled the streets at night, calling out the hour and hoping that their vociferous presence would be sufficient to deter any potential criminals. In the rural areas the parish constables were mainly concerned with the execution of warrants and the serving of summonses.

These ill-trained, often unfit and uneducated men were easy prey for determined criminals and other ruffians and their lot was indeed not a happy one. In fact, any representative of authority was liable to violent abuse – poor law overseers, gamekeepers, beadles – all were popular targets. An early survey of assaults in Bedfordshire revealed that of 250 recorded assaults, 34 (14 per cent) were directed against constables or poor law overseers while a similar number of gamekeepers and other servants were victims.

Constables were generally unpopular with the lower social orders, many of whom were often either involved in criminal activities themselves or aided and abetted those who were. Given the bleak conditions under which these people lived, this fact is not surprising and the comment is not intended in any way as being critical or disparaging. An example of this antipathy towards the representatives of law and order may be found in an 1825 case in which two young men stole pistols from some Yeomanry troopers. The local constable attended and detained the miscreants but had great difficulty in holding on to his prisoners, being violently assaulted by the villagers who made no bones about siding with the thieves.

In the summer of 1827, Constable Thomas Franklin of Leighton Buzzard was called to an ale house where a violent quarrel was taking place. One witness later stated:

> ... I saw the said John Brandon strike the said constable twice, bang full in the face. The blows knocked the constable down on his back [and] John Brandon fell down with him ... The constable appeared to be very much hurt and his face was all over blood.[12]

Hostility towards the representatives of law and order was not confined to this type of bodily harm, grievous though it may often have been. When Henry Thompson of Ruardean (Gloucestershire) arrested a woman in possession of stolen wheat in 1817, her husband William Turner shot the constable dead.

The formation of the Metropolitan Police in 1829 saw a great change in policing methods, standards and styles but made little difference to the attitudes of the general public towards the enforcement of the growing amount of legislation aimed at suppressing 'idle and disorderly persons' and 'rogues and vagabonds', all of whom were from the lower social strata. At the other end of the scale, the landowning gentry saw the trend towards a greatly enlarged police service as irrelevant. This New Police merely represented an additional burden to be borne by them in the form of increased taxation. Only the middle class, the shopkeepers and small businessmen, welcomed the improved and enlarged policing initiatives, especially in the burgeoning urban areas where the lower orders were proving an impediment to their capitalistic endeavours.

All the resentment which had been directed against the watchmen and Bow Street Runners in the capital was now turned towards this new, and to many, unwelcome, manifestation of the ruling classes' authority. In 1830, the year following the creation of the force, two constables lost their lives; Constable Joseph Grantham was beaten to death in the June of that year while attempting to make an arrest and became the holder of the dubious distinction of being the first Metropolitan Policeman to be killed on duty. In August, Constable John Long was stabbed in the chest with a razor-sharp cobbler's knife during a check on three suspicious persons and died instantly.

The antipathy of the working classes to this new, repressive force was manifested in numerous public meetings, advertised in an astonishingly virulent and inflamatory manner, calling upon the people to resist these

> ... Raw Lobsters, Blue Devils, Or by whatever appropriate name they be known ... a Force unknown to the British Constitution and called into existence by a Parliament illegally constituted, legislating for their individual interests, consequently in opposition to the Public good.

One protest meeting was called for 12 May 1833 at Coldbath Fields, Clerkenwell, and the handbills publicizing this event encouraged those attending to come armed. Rabble-rousing speeches were made and the waiting police, numbering some 600, were ordered to break up the meeting. Outnumbered ten to one and facing a fearsome array of weapons ranging from knives, improvised lances, brickbats and cudgels, the police suffered heavy casualties and one, Constable Robert Culley, was killed by a stab wound to the chest.

At the subsequent inquest, a verdict of justifiable homicide was returned on the grounds that the Riot Act had not been read nor had the people been advised to disperse, and that the conduct of the police had been ferocious, brutal and unprovoked. The jurymen were fêted as heroes by the populace, each being given a silver loving cup and treated to a boat trip up the Medway river.

The jury's verdict was subsequently overturned by the King's Bench Division of the High Court but the argument festered on. William Cobbett, MP for Oldham, was particularly clamorous in his complaints about the use of uniformed peace officers in a military manner. He alleged that these men had carried firearms and swords but this allegation is not supported by any of the injuries suffered by the rioters.

One reason for much of this violence was the fact that a great deal of the increasing legislation in early Victorian times was aimed at 'improving' the poor by curtailing their access to drink and the possibilities for gaming. But these were the traditional pastimes of the poor; the downtrodden masses enjoyed their tipple to the extent of frequently anaesthetizing themselves to their miserable condition by becoming paralytically drunk. Their only opportunity for increasing their meagre income was often seen to lie in the prospect of winning a substantial wager (winnings which might be spent on food and warm clothing but, more likely, on further ale and gin). The efforts of the police and other officials to enforce these laws met with sturdy resistance and there was often serious friction between the opposing sides. 'Police constables were violently assaulted when on their beats throughout the [nineteenth] century.'[13]

By the 1840s a clear ebb and flow could be distinguished in the attitudes of the public and press towards London's police. Suspicion and resentment followed each violent demonstration or riot which the police put down with extreme firmness, while any death of a policeman on duty was inevitably followed by a wave of sympathy and demands for them to be better protected and for firearms to be issued to them for their protection. A typical case was that involving Thomas Cooper, an ardent collector and user of firearms who is said to have dispatched all the cats in his neighbourhood in Clerkenwell. One afternoon in May 1842 Cooper was seen by a constable, carrying a cavalry pistol in each hand. Although he attempted to hide, he was flushed out by the Constable and, when the latter asked him to account for his behaviour, Cooper fired at the officer's head, wounding him in the arm which he had raised to protect his face. Cooper tried to discharge the second pistol at the Constable but it misfired. Although he grappled with the offender, the Constable was too weak from loss of blood to do much but the chase was taken up by a colleague who had heard the shots. This officer, Constable Mallett, was joined by a number of ordinary citizens and a regular hue and cry followed, augmented shortly afterwards by Constable Daley. The latter, in company with two of the pursuing citizens, caught up with Cooper who shot one of the pursuers in the shoulder and then shot Constable Daley through the heart at point blank range, killing him instantly. With both pistols now discharged and no opportunity to reload, Cooper surrendered to his pursuers and was eventually tried, convicted and executed.

This incident pushed aside all allegations of police brutality and many newspapers asked why the police were not equipped with cutlasses or firearms, ridiculing the presumption that a policeman could protect himself against an armed desperado with just a short piece of lignum vitae.

However, it must not be thought that, because the Metropolitan Police was confined to the capital, there were no problems elsewhere. The great upheavals caused by the Industrial Revolution led to unprecedented population movements, in particular a migration towards the urban centres of industry. The insatiable demands for power made by these industries led to the coalfields being under increasing pressure and continually seeking further labour. In particular, the coalfields of South Wales and Durham were reported as attracting large numbers of 'escaped criminals and dissolute people' and the pit strike which took place in 1831–32 was noted for its ferocity. After the creation of county constabularies policemen were often assaulted in the pit villages where they were viewed with great disfavour as 'the bosses' lackies'. It is true that the police were often used to facilitate the use of blacklegs and assisted in the eviction of sacked pit workers.

Throughout the nineteenth century assaults on the police formed a significant proportion of the recorded assaults (although it has to be accepted that the police were duty bound to report an assault on their person whereas a similarly injured civilian might overlook the incident or determine to get his own back in other ways). One worrying factor was the ready availability of shotguns and fowling pieces in the rural areas which led to numerous cases of pot-shots being taken at policemen and gamekeepers.

In the two decades between 1830 and 1850 no fewer than 32 policemen met their death through criminal activity in places as far apart as London and Liverpool, Brighton and Bathampton, Kendal and Kent, Shropshire and Suffolk, usually being either shot, stabbed or beaten to death. Around half of these died in riots or other disturbances such as pub brawls, while the remainder of the cases related to attempted arrests for crime or the checking of suspects. Of these 32 officers, seven were shot dead and these murders were invariably committed in a rural area or small market town such as Saffron Walden or Ashton-under-Lyne. It is interesting to note at this point that during the equivalent period one century later (1930–50) the number of policemen killed (excluding those who died as a result of enemy action during the war) was 17 or little more than half the number who died in the earlier period.

The dangers to which the police were exposed resulted in individual officers frequently using a great deal of discretion. One constable who joined the Metropolitan Police in 1855 recalled allowing a fight to continue uninterrupted in a cul-de-sac of slum houses occupied by poor Irishmen, having been warned that one of his predecessors had been murdered when he ventured into the same street, an early example of a 'no-go area'.[14]

The second half of the nineteenth century saw the completion of the plan to provide a police force for every part of the country: an 1856 Act of Parliament requiring all county authorities which had not so far done so to create a county constabulary to cover those parts of their shire which were not served by a borough or city police force. This period also saw a gradual lessening of the political disorders of the previous half-century, while the veterans of the Crimean War found themselves being somewhat better looked after than their predecessors from the Napoleonic War (albeit very poorly served by modern standards) and thus the need for them to resort to crime in order to live was not so great.

However, this did not mean that violent assaults on the police were any fewer and the unlawful killing of policemen continued unabated. Whereas in the first 20 years of organized policing (1829–50) deaths of policemen amounted on average to 1.6 per annum, in the second half of the century the average was nearly 1.9 per annum. However, it must be admitted that the numbers of policemen increased dramatically during this time and therefore one cannot draw a fair comparison.

As in the early part of the century, assaults on police were proportionally greater than the average, with some 15 per cent of all summary prosecutions for assault in the 1860s and about 21 per cent in the 1890s being for attacks on police officers. Most of these were probably minor and, once again, the likelihood of policemen being more conscientious in reporting minor assaults must be borne in mind. Nevertheless, it is clear that in the last quarter of the nineteenth century there was an epidemic of burglaries carried out by armed, professional and determined burglars, including the likes of the infamous Charlie Peace, and giving rise to a great deal of public concern. This manifested itself in proposals in the press that armed burglars should be flogged when caught, although this time there were few suggestions that the police should be similarly provided with firearms.

Even one hundred years ago, the influence of undesirable literature was blamed for the escalation of violence, the father of Ernest Castles, charged with murdering a constable in Oldham, claiming that his mind had been corrupted by the reading of trashy literature. This was, of course, a time when there were a great many lurid magazines relating 'true crime' stories and tales such as 'Maria Martin or the Murder in the Red Barn' were widely read by those seeking a vicarious thrill.

The dawning of a new century gave rise to hopes for a new morality and a crime-free society – hopes which were obviously doomed to disappointment. Even the 'world fit for heroes to live in' envisaged after the Great War failed to become a reality although social conditions were slowly improving and bore little resemblance to those which existed a century earlier.

Nevertheless, the police still had their problems. In the early years of the new century no fewer than 2,500 Metropolitan policemen were reported to have been injured annually as a result of assault – about 15 per cent of the whole force. Unofficial figures suggest that perhaps one in four London policemen were assaulted each year. Many of these assaults took place in particular areas; Whitechapel was especially notorious for the way its inhabitants 'considered they had a natural right to get fighting drunk and knock a policeman about whenever the spirit moved them'.[15] Campbell Bank in Islington was another black spot, popularly known as 'Kill Copper Row' and no Metropolitan policeman relished patrolling that area at night in the inter-war years.[16]

Similar problems existed in parts of other industrial towns, such as those in Lancashire. While investigating an assault on another constable at a steel works in Newton Heath, James Bent was savagely beaten and burned with red-hot irons. And the rural areas were not exempt; in some of these constables adopted the habit of carrying a stout walking stick when they made their patrols, this being regarded as better protection than the comparatively short and light truncheon with which they were issued.

The period from 1900 to 1939 was a comparatively quiet one so far as serious assaults on the police were concerned. A total of 37 officers lost their lives through criminal acts, firearms being involved in more than half these cases – a much higher proportion than in the 1830–50 period referred to earlier. An incident which occurred at Great Yarmouth in 1909 is fairly typical of these: Constable Charles Alger was 37 and had been a constable in the Great Yarmouth Police for the preceding 14 years. He was a solid, reliable type and was well respected. During the afternoon of 18 August, he was sent by his inspector to deal with a complaint about a man beating his wife (a not too uncommon occurrence in some districts in those days). On his arrival Constable Alger saw Thomas Allen, a known ruffian, standing in the garden of his house. On seeing the Constable, Allen bent down and produced a sawn-off shotgun from the potato bed and fired at the unfortunate officer at point-blank range. With severe wounds to the face and neck, Constable Alger died almost instantaneously. The offender was later arrested by other officers, tried and sentenced to death. He was, however, later reprieved on the grounds of insanity.

Despite all this, the reminiscences of former policemen as well as the available statistics tend to suggest that the first half of the twentieth century was not marred by the same degree of violence against them as had been the case where their predecessors were concerned. Drink still figured prominently in many of these assaults on the police; Saturday night punch-ups were commonplace and all too often the beat policeman found himself drawn into the fracas while trying to restore order. Even in the 1920s certain districts remained highly dangerous to the conscientious policeman, prompting the magistrate at the Thames Police Court to comment:

> Some people go in for parson-baiting and others go in for baiting the police ... I hold no brief for the police but it is dirty and cowardly for a gang to set upon one or two men. It is not English or decent. The people in this district must be taught to find some other amusement ... there are always the pictures.[17]

Throughout the years, the violence directed against the police has stemmed from two, or possibly three, main sources: assaults by criminals of all sorts, usually in the attempt to avoid apprehension, and then assaults arising out of disturbances – which may again be divided into the riot or political rally/demonstration type of event and the small-scale affray or pub brawl. The pub brawl seems to have declined over the years but the post-war years have seen no reduction in the numbers of demonstrations, many of which turned particularly nasty and developed into full-scale riots. The 'Ban the Bomb' demonstrations which were a feature of the 1960s and early 1970s were generally free from serious disorder, but the picture changed and became more extremely political and violent soon afterwards. Perhaps the beginnings of the more violent demonstration may be traced back to the Red Lion Square demonstration in 1974 described earlier. During the National Front rally in Lewisham three years later two policemen were stabbed, fortunately without fatal results.

The weapons used against the police continued to be the fist/boot, the knife and, increasingly, the gun. In the nineteenth century (or at least the last 70 years of that century), a total of 32 policemen were killed by the criminal use of firearms – usually a shotgun. This type of weapon was readily available, especially in the rural areas and firearms control was lax. Most nineteenth-century firearms legislation, such as the 1870 Gun Licence Act, was more concerned with the fiscal possibilities than with the criminal use of such weapons. Licences under this Act were issued by the Commissioners of Inland Revenue who saw the proliferation of weapons as a good source of revenue rather than a public order problem.

Two attempts were made, in 1881 and 1883, to legislate against the carrying of hand guns in a public place but, reflecting the current American experience, both of these failed on the ground that an Englishman had a fundamental right to carry a firearm for his personal protection.

The gaps in the scope of this Act led to the passing in 1903 of the Pistols Act, but firearms were generally controlled in a lackadaisical way until the passing of the first Firearms Act which prohibited certain weapons (such as machine guns and gas pistols) and imposed strict, police supervised controls on other weapons (excluding shotguns). Because of the sporting connection, shotgun control remained essentially a fiscal matter and the issuing of licences for this type of weapon was subject to much less stringent conditions.

It is because of the more ready availability of these sporting weapons that the sawn-off shotgun became a popular weapon for criminals. Being subject to strict controls, revolvers and automatics are much more difficult to obtain than a shotgun, and consequently illicit sales of such weapons command a much higher price. And a shotgun is just as effective and just as deadly as a hand gun and, with the barrel shortened (and often the butt as well) nearly as easily concealed and handled. In the period from 1900 to 1970, the number of police officers killed by the use of firearms reached 43 – an increase of one-third over the preceding 70 years. By the time we reach 1994, the figure for the whole of the century so far has jumped to 64.

In recent years these traditional weapons have been supplemented by the favourite weapon of the international terrorist – the bomb. Three Metropolitan police officers, including one woman officer, were killed by a terrorist bomb in 1983 and, in recent years, two civilian explosives officers working for the police have died when the device they were attempting to disarm went off. Yet another new weapon is the motor car. There have been a number of cases where a policeman has been killed by a motor car, usually accidentally. Probably the first of these occurred in Folkestone in 1908 when Constable Frederick Nash was knocked down. The driver was charged with manslaughter but was acquitted. Over the ensuing years 17 vehicle drivers were charged with the manslaughter of policemen but there was no allegation that the killing was intentional in any of these cases. But this is not so where the driver is alleged to have deliberately run down the officer. As early as 1930, Constable Arthur Lawes of the Metropolitan Police was run down by a stolen car in what was deemed to be a criminal act. Since then there have been 11 further cases of the deliberate use of a motor vehicle to kill a police officer.

The current view is that, over the past 20 years or so, the police have been increasingly exposed to violence, including that resulting in fatalities. Statistics tend to support the general trend towards the use of violence, although once again we have to keep in mind both the increased number of policemen and policewomen and the readiness of these – prompted by such factors as the possibility of criminal charges, compensation and pension rights – to report any injury suffered by them. This is not meant as criticism; it is merely mentioned to keep things in perspective. Nevertheless, during 1994 guns were used against police officers in London on 41 occasions, in one case a sub-machine gun being used. In Strathclyde, Kalashnikov rifles have been used by drug traffickers to protect their deals. Even in peaceful, rural West Mercia, police were called to no fewer than 31 firearms incidents, 12 of which involved direct confrontation with armed criminals.

Statistics concerning the brandishing or firing of firearms by criminals are notoriously unreliable but, where an unfortunate policeman or woman has been killed by a criminal act, the facts are somewhat clearer. For the purpose of comparison, during the period 1830 to 1899 126 police officers were killed in this manner (plus a further five where there was insufficient evidence to proceed with a charge of murder or manslaughter). In the whole of the twentieth century thus far 124 fatalities have been recorded (plus 13 cases

where there was insufficient evidence), which suggests
that the twentieth century has been *less* violent so far
as the police are concerned than the previous century.
However, if these figures are broken down into
decades, one sees that the lower figure for this century
is due to exceptionally low numbers in the early and
(especially) middle years of the period. In every year
since an all-time low in the 1931–40 decade, figures
have generally risen steadily, peaking in the 1980s.
Whether the 1990s will see this progression continuing
remains to be seen.

TABLE 1
TOTAL NUMBER OF POLICE OFFICERS KILLED BY
CRIMINAL ACTS IN EACH DECADE

1830–40	12	(2)*	1901–10	12	(6)	1971–80	15	(7)
1841–50	20	(5)	1911–20	11	(7)	1981–90	25	(12)
1851–60	10	(2)	1921–30	10	(6)	1991–94	9†	(2)
1861–70	20	(5)	1931–40	6	(2)			
1871–80	26	(6)	1941–50	9	(4)			
1881–90	20	(10)	1951–60	11	(9)			
1891–1900	20	(5)	1961–70	14	(9)			

Notes
* Figures in brackets indicate those cases where firearms were used.
† This figure may be extrapolated to 22/23 by the end of the decade.

Although it is not the purpose of this book to find
reasons for these variations, it is interesting to note
that, in the 1920s and especially the 1930s, at a time of
great economic depression and joblessness, when there
was a natural antipathy towards government and
towards authority in general, and when crime could be
expected to be rife, the number of police officers killed
was at an all-time low. Even during the war years when
morals were lax and firearms often readily available

the number of policemen killed was remarkably low.[18]

It is also politic to keep in mind the fact that, although undoubtedly a dangerous job, and one which appears to be becoming increasingly so, policing figures comparatively low on the list of occupations with an exceptional level of deaths or injuries. According to the Home Office/Health and Safety Executive figures for 1993, 63 construction workers, 16 agricultural workers, 11 engineering workers and seven miners lost their lives, as against two police officers. Coal mining recorded the highest number of injuries per 100,000 workers: 3,933. Postal workers, builders and vehicle manufacturers all recorded more than 1,500 per 100,000, as against 1,333 police. The main difference in all these statistics is that the deaths and injuries suffered by police officers were more often than not deliberately inflicted while those in the other professions were injured or killed through entirely accidental circumstances.

In order to parry any allegations of sexual discrimination, it is perhaps important to stress that the repeated references to policemen so far have been deliberate, since the first woman officer to have been killed by criminal acts appears to have been WPC Mandy Rayner of the Hertfordshire Police who was killed during a vehicle chase in 1982. Since then two Metropolitan women police officers have been killed by terrorist activities: WPC Jane Arbuthnot (by bomb in 1983) and WPC Yvonne Fletcher (shot outside the Libyan Embassy in 1984).

It is generally accepted that there is today an increased readiness on the part of certain criminals to resort to firearms; in the Metropolitan Police Area alone the police were confronted with firearms on 59 occasions in the period from March 1994 to March 1995 – a 30 per cent rise over the previous year. This is not to mention various other lethal weapons, especially knives, and the subject for debate is whether the routine arming of the police would better protect both the officers themselves and the public in general or, in fact, lead to an escalation in the levels of violence and add to the risks for innocent bystanders.

3 Pistol-packing policemen

Although the image of the British police is invariably one of an unarmed force, this is not, and never has been, the complete and true picture.

Long before the formation of the Metropolitan Police in 1829 there was a City Watch in London but this, consisting largely of elderly paupers or labourers working as watchmen during the night after their day's work, is generally regarded as having been ineffective or corrupt or both. There were 18 different police authorities within the parish of St. Pancras alone, while the whole of Kennington was guarded by three watchmen of whom it was reported that one was drunk all the time and the other two most of the time. Many London parishes, including Fulham, Ealing, Wandsworth, Stratford and Bow were without watchmen of any sort.[19] A small section was taken from this largely ineffective body to patrol the city streets and in 1791 was given a uniform for the first time. The number gradually increased until by 1824 there were 24 men, half of whom worked at night and the other half by day.

Meanwhile, the Fielding brothers were experimenting with main road patrols in an effort to stamp out the menace of highwaymen and footpads and by the 1790s they had an *armed* patrol of around 70 determined men, based at Bow Street Magistrates' Court, patrolling the main roads leading to the centre of London every night. These Bow Street Runners were so successful (as compared with the inefficient City Watch) that by 1828 the organization had developed to consist of a Horse Patrol of 60 men, a 100-strong Dismounted Patrol, a Night Foot Patrol of a similar size and a small (27) Day Foot Patrol. Their success was largely due to the fact that they were paid by results, their main remuneration being the rewards offered for wanted criminals. Such a system was, of course, open to corruption, and there is no doubt that a number of these law-enforcement officers were corrupt or were themselves involved in crime. Being but a loosely controlled body, there was little in the way of standard equipment and most therefore armed themselves as they thought fit. A cutlass was commonly carried while many also armed themselves with a brace of horse pistols.

For various reasons which do not need to be rehearsed here, there was growing dissatisfaction with these thief takers and, despite considerable opposition from those who saw any form of police as a duplication of the despised French system with its spies and informers, the Metropolitan Police was formed in 1829 with just over 1,000 men. Within a year or so the New Police, as it was often called, could boast some 2,000 men, all of whom were generally unarmed apart from a truncheon, although a stock of swords and belts had been obtained from Mr Tatham of Charing Cross as well as rattles, staves and handbolts purchased from another supplier. This stock was supplemented later the same year because of the increased number of constables enrolled and the opportunity was taken to purchase 50 pairs of pistols. These were flintlocks, sometimes referred to as the 'police model' as they were expressly made for the Metropolitan Police, but they were not issued to patrolling officers as a matter of routine.

As has been mentioned previously, not all the citizens of London were favourably disposed towards the police and the early constables were subjected to a great deal of violence, especially in certain areas. In some outer London districts and in a few rough, working-class areas, the constables regularly patrolled armed with cutlasses (sabres in the case of mounted patrols). An incident in 1830 during which Constable Berry was both shot and stabbed while attempting to arrest two burglars aroused considerable sympathy, however, and the residents of Tulse Hill petitioned the Commissioner, calling for the police in the neighbourhood to be furnished with a sword or cutlass and at least one pistol each: 'We are decidedly of the opinion that had Policeman Berry been armed with the above weapons he would have taken both ruffians into safe custody without having been so barbarously attacked.' In response to this petition, the Home Secretary agreed, somewhat surprisingly, that 'each Police Officer in the district should be provided with a cutlass for his defence.' The standard police cutlass, to which this refers, would have been carried while on night duty only.

Although considerable stress has always been placed on the non-military and civilian nature of the British police, the early forces were nevertheless organized on a bureaucratic and hierarchical basis. The first Commissioners of the Metropolitan Police and most if not all the county chief constables were former military men and the officers under their command were subjected to a strict discipline code. Some county forces, notably that in Essex, adopted a very military-style of policing and in every force the men were drilled and required to indulge in 'spit and polish' like their counterparts in the Army, being expected to be well turned out at all times. It is true that, unlike the private soldier, the individual members of these 'civilian' police forces were able to exercise a considerable degree of discretion but, as has been pointed out by other writers, so too did the Prussian *Schutzmann* who was certainly not a civilian

37

(invariably ex-army) and who patrolled wearing an impressive spiked helmet and armed to the teeth. The main difference lay in the national cultures; had there been rather more violence employed by members of organizations such as the Chartists and a little less reticence on the part of the Home Office, it is quite possible that the early British police would have been armed like their continental counterparts and we should have inherited a police force which carried pistols as a matter of routine.

However, although frequently armed with a cutlass, there was still no question of an issue of firearms to the police. Indeed, the Commissioner instructed that 'Superintendents are to take particular care that the Constables do not carry Pistols about with them, nor in fact Arms of any kind without the express permission of the Commissioner thereto'. Paradoxically, members of the public were not prohibited at this time from carrying arms for their personal protection and so the police were less well protected than some members of the public.

The Bow Street Mounted Patrol, which had controlled the main highways into London and provided a measure of protection against the scourge of the highwayman since its reconstitution in 1805, was not abolished when the Metropolitan Police was formed and continued to work in parallel with the new force for seven years. In 1836 it was renamed the Mounted Police and transferred *en bloc* to the Metropolitan Police. The 73 men of this body comprised mainly ex-cavalrymen and formed the first truly uniformed and armed police in London. Their blue coat with yellow buttons, bright red waistcoat and black leather boots, hat and stock were in stark contrast to the civilian-style, blue swallow-tailed coats, white duck trousers and black stove-pipe hats of the early Metropolitan constables. And their weapons, consisting of a sabre, a pistol and a truncheon, were incomparably better than those of their new colleagues. It was presumably thought that these highway patrolmen were at greater risk than their urban counterparts since they were permitted to retain their pistols for at least the next 30 years and their sabres until 1868. Over the years the stock of pistols issued to the mounted branch and held available for issue to other members of the Metropolitan Police as necessary was updated. In 1844 a new, single-shot, percussion belt pistol was purchased with the novel addition of paper cartridges instead of separate ball, powder and wad. There was, however, no facility for reloading once the single shot had been discharged.

Similarly, when the Thames Police, formed in 1798 to combat thefts from riverside docks and warehouses, was amalgamated into the Metropolitan Police in 1839 as the Thames Division, they retained their personal cutlasses and a number of naval-type pistols, although their fearsome arsenal of blunderbusses was surrendered.

In the early years, the Metropolitan Police was often called upon to quell disorders in provincial towns where there was no or an inadequate police force, usually working alongside the military. The superiority of these new policemen was expressed by Edwin Chadwick, an ardent police reformer, who wrote:

> the private soldier has both his hands occupied with a musket with which ... the inflicting of death [is] by firing or stabbing. The constable or police-man, whose weapon is a truncheon or, on desperate occasions, the cutlass, has one hand at liberty to seize and hold his prisoner whilst with the other he represses by force.[20]

The success of the Metropolitan Police prompted many other cities to form their own force while a number of influential people advocated the formation of a national, well-trained 'general constabulary, *armed* and trained on the Irish model'.[21] This point of view was supported by Captain W. C. Harris, the Chief Constable of the newly formed Hampshire Constabulary. As a former light infantry officer, he did not believe that the arming of his men would have a detrimental effect on relations with the public, although he added the proviso that arms should only be issued if invasion were threatened.[22]

The debate on whether or not the police should carry weapons was a lively one through the years. The *Police Service Advertiser*, which first appeared in 1866, carried much correspondence on the question. In 1869 a serious spate of grave-robbing in London led to the formation of a 'graveyard patrol', the members of which patrolled the burial grounds, armed with a cutlass, but there was still no question of their carrying firearms and these remained an infrequent issue. Even when the Fenian Brotherhood, sworn to liberate Ireland from the English yoke, embarked upon a campaign of bombing and shooting in 1867, shooting dead Sergeant Charles Brett of the Manchester Police, the Metropolitan Police response was to arrange for officers to receive cutlass training at Wellington Barracks. Just how these weapons were intended to combat the use of the bomb and the gun is not clear.

Such was the threat of Fenian activity that in 1862 the Chief Constable of Lancashire ordered that no firearms were to be kept at police stations in the county. This somewhat curious decision was designed to prevent members of this illegal organization from attacking the stations and taking the weapons by force. However, two years later he had to rescind this order and issue 20 revolvers. The wisdom of this later decision was demonstrated in Manchester in 1867 when Fenian supporters attacked a police escort and helped some of their colleagues to escape. In the mêlée which accompanied this rescue, the unfortunate Sergeant Brett was shot and killed. When three Fenians were subsequently hanged in Manchester, 25 armed policemen were seconded from the county force to assist their city colleagues. Fortunately they did not have to use their weapons.

By this time the old-fashioned pistols, powder flasks and bullet moulds had been withdrawn from the Metropolitan Police and the force borrowed some revolvers from the Army and a few officers were instructed in their use. These borrowed weapons were replaced in the following August (1868) by the purchase of 622 Adams's breech-loading revolvers from the Tower of London, probably ex-Army issue. These firearms were distributed round the London police stations with a strict instruction that 'Superintendents are to see that they are kept under lock and key in a safe place'. The result of this injunction was that these firearms were seldom issued for use, even when the circumstances clearly justified this course of action and despite pleas from the night-duty constables who faced armed and determined burglars. This fact was brought forcibly home in 1881 by the murder of Constable Frederick Atkins who was shot when he disturbed a burglar. The perpetrator of this crime was never found but the result was astonishing; more than 1,500 policemen attended the funeral, while local tradesmen closed their premises as a mark of respect. The press clamoured for better protection for these vulnerable officers and the Home Secretary was constrained to ask the new Commissioner Colonel Henderson whether his men wished to be issued with firearms. The Commissioner consulted his superintendents who were unanimously opposed to the idea, claiming that such a move would be highly detrimental to police/public relationships. They added that their constables were of a similar point of view.

The Home Secretary was apparently unconvinced by this assertion and called for fuller reports, including the views of the inspectors. This further survey was carried out shortly afterwards and the Commissioner reported that the men were of the opinion that a revolver would not afford much protection. He added that there was a danger of a constable being prosecuted if he used such a weapon with deadly effect (although this contention was somewhat diluted by the admission that the same argument could be applied to the use of the truncheon). This report from the Commissioner was followed two days later by yet another murder of a policeman (Constable George Cole, by a burglar).

The Home Secretary responded that a summary of these fuller reports, 'which embrace the opinion of the inspectors who are more likely to be acquainted with the real sentiments of the men', had convinced him that the view previously reported to him by the Commissioner was erroneous and that there was a widespread and general dissatisfaction in the Police with 'the present means furnished them for self-defence'.

Highlighting the Commissioner's apparent complacency, the press were virtually unanimous in their espousal of the call to arms, although some still questioned whether such a move would lead to an escalation in the use of firearms by criminals. The *Evening Standard* voiced the opinion that:

> ... Parliament ... entirely overlooks the really urgent problems of the day. One of these is the manner in which persons who meditate a crime arm themselves with revolvers ... It is not only foolish but absolutely cruel to send Policemen out to combat men possessed with revolvers without any other arm than a short club. If the law will not protect the Police by heavy

penalties from armed resistance, they should at least have weapons to enable them to defend their lives.[23]

On the same day, the *St James's Gazette* noted that 'burglars now commonly carry revolvers and policemen ... are entirely at their mercy', but went on to suggest that 'arming of the Police would be an un-English proceeding and would perhaps still further brutalize the burglar.'

Paradoxically, the greatest problems were being experienced not, as one might have expected, in central London or the East End but in the more genteel suburbs. The reason for this was, of course, that business premises in the City were well protected while there was very little to be stolen in the poorer, working-class areas. The best and easiest pickings for a burglar were the middle-class villas which had sprung up in the booming London suburbs.

The Commissioner felt constrained to examine the matter further and in 1883 instructed every sergeant and constable serving on an outer division to submit a report as to whether he would wish to carry a firearm or not. The response was quite astonishing; out of a total of 6,325 no fewer than 4,430 asked to be issued with a revolver. The advice of Scotland Yard's legal adviser, the barrister James Edward Davis, was sought and his opinion set out the circumstances under which a police constable might lawfully use a firearm:

1. In self-defence, where he cannot reasonably otherwise defend himself;
2. Where a person is committing or attempting to commit murder if necessary to prevent to completion of the crime;
3. In cases of burglary or robbery with violence where the offender does not desist after being required to do so by the Constable, who has warned him that he will fire;

43

4. Where after committing an offence in (2) or (3) the offender flees the Constable may use the revolver to disable him after warning him, if no other lawful means of effecting the arrest are open to the Constable;
5. Where a person, not necessarily having committed an offence, fires on the Constable or manifests such an intention, the Constable will be justified in using his revolver;
6. There will be no justification for the use of a firearm where the offence was not committed recently. Should the offender offer armed resistance then the provisions of (1) might apply.

These conditions have been paraphrased for the sake of convenience but they give a reasonable indication of the legal position as seen by counsel. This was supplemented at the Commissioner's request by a further opinion as to the legality of using firearms to prevent a prison break; the lawyer believed that where anyone was attempting to gain entry to a prison in order to effect the release of an inmate, a constable might, after giving due warning, fire on the offender. Where there was no time for such a warning to be given, such as when the offender was about to detonate an explosive device, the constable might fire without warning.

As a result of this second opinion Home Office permission was given for the arming of the police on duty at Millbank Prison (where Fenian prisoners were held), other than those constables 'employed in the public thoroughfare'. The Commissioner was not prepared, however, to take the responsibility of recommending to the Home Secretary that he should issue an order that the police should in future carry revolvers when employed on night duty in the outer districts. He was prepared to go only so far as to suggest that it might be possible to issue revolvers to those men who wanted to have them when on night duty in the outer divisions and who, in the opinion of their superiors, could be trusted to use them with discretion.

The Home Secretary replied that he was prepared to accede to this latter suggestion and authorize the carrying of revolvers by policemen on night duty in the suburban divisions; but such men were to be strictly enjoined that the revolver was only to be used for self-defence as described in item 1 of Mr Davis's opinion, and not for any of the other grounds described.

This meant that, for the first time, police officers had the same rights of self-defence as the rest of the populace; but there remained considerable resistance to the initiative from the hierarchy, including a few superintendents who appeared to fear the repercussions which could fall on their shoulders in the event of a firearm's being used by one of their men.

The reality of having armed police on the streets had the result of cooling the interest manifested by the press in the subject. The *Daily Telegraph* published an editorial which suggested that 'to arm our Police Force ... with six-shooters is a kind of desperate resource which does not recommend itself to an impartial judgment ... The risks of inconsiderate shooting are far too great to allow for this particular remedy against murderous depredators.'[24]

Perhaps surprisingly, even the *Police Review*, which first appeared in 1893 and provided a forum for correspondence on the subject, came down on the side of the advocates of the status quo. The editor, John Kempster, was adamant that the police should *not* be armed: 'for whenever the preventive arm is sharpened thus the desperate hand of crime rises, with a deadlier weapon, to the occasion ... If the burglar feels all right with his jemmy, let us not force on him a revolver.'[25]

In just ten years the pendulum had swung across to the opposite point of view and, now that the prospect of armed policemen on the streets of London was becoming a reality, many were having second thoughts. Given the lack of training undergone by the men to be issued with these weapons, there was perhaps some justification for the reservations being expressed in many quarters.

Nevertheless, on 16 October 1883 the Commissioner received formal permission from the Home Office to issue revolvers to the constables on night duty in the outer divisions. These revolvers were to be of the new, lighter type, and an order was subsequently placed with Philip Webley & Son of Birmingham for 931 centre-fire, 0.450-calibre revolvers, a type which became known as the Metropolitan Police model. The failure of the Adams Company to obtain the contract, despite significant price cutting, was a serious blow to its status and one from which it never really recovered.

The new weapons began to arrive in the early months of 1884 and an instruction was hurriedly issued in the form of a police order on 30 June 1884. In view of the importance of this unprecedented step, the order is reproduced below in full:

THE FOLLOWING REGULATIONS RELATING TO THE ISSUE TO, AND THE USE BY POLICE OF REVOLVERS, HAVING BEEN APPROVED, THE SUPERINTENDENTS ARE TO SEE THAT THEY ARE STRICTLY ADHERED TO

1. Revolvers are only to be issued to men who desire to have them when employed on night duty, and who can, in the opinion of the Divisional Officer, be trusted to use them with discretion.
2. Revolvers are to be kept at the Stations to which men who are to use them are attached, the Officers on duty thereat being held responsible for their safe custody and efficient condition.
3. A revolver is to be issued to a Constable on

parading for duty, on his own application only, at the time of parading. It is to be loaded by the Officer parading the relief, and placed in a holster. An entry is then to be made in the Occurrence Book showing the name and number of the Constable to whom a revolver has been issued, also the number of the revolver.

4. The revolver is to be carried in a holster on the belt on the right side in front of the truncheon, and is not to be taken out of the holster for any purpose whatsoever, except in self defence.

5. Officers carrying revolvers are to be strictly enjoined that they are only to be used in self defence where there is a necessity for resorting to their use, as when a Constable is attacked by a person with firearms or other deadly weapon and cannot otherwise reasonably protect himself, a Constable (as a private person also) may resort to a revolver as a means of defence.

6. On going off duty, the Officer in charge of the station is to receive the revolvers from the Police, and in their presence extract the cartridges, carefully examine both the weapon and cartridges and make an entry in the Occurrence Book of the condition in which they are delivered to him.

7. The Officer having the use of a revolver is to report, on going off duty, every instance in which he has had occasion to remove it from its holster during his tour of duty, whether it was used or not. Such reports are to be dealt with as 'Urgent' and submitted at once to the Commissioner through the District Superintendent.

8. Before a revolver is issued to an Officer, he is to be properly instructed in its use, and a report of his competency submitted through District Superintendents to the Commissioner for his approval.

It will be noted that only the first of Mr Davis's recommendations – that of the use of firearms for self-protection – had been retained and incorporated in paragraph 5 of the new police instructions.

Despite the forebodings expressed in many quarters, the fact that a number of Metropolitan policemen were patrolling the outer London area with a revolver at the ready did not produce any disastrous results. The streets were not littered with the bodies of burglars or, more to the point, innocent bystanders. What is interesting is the fact that for the rest of the century only one Metropolitan policeman (Detective-Sergeant Joseph Joyce) was shot dead by a criminal, while other, less fortunate officers met their end through the criminal use of firearms in places as far apart as Cumberland, Essex, the West Riding (two), Durham, the North Riding, Wiltshire, Middlesbrough and Inverness-shire. Whether one may infer from this that the well-publicized practice of carrying a firearm gave the Metropolitan officers a substantial measure of protection is a matter for debate, but the circumstantial evidence certainly points to this, especially when one considers the size of the Metropolitan Police force at that time in comparison with the size of the forces in the rest of the country. It is true that policemen, both in London and in the provinces, were faced with firearms on a number of occasions and were not infrequently shot at and sometimes wounded, but as the relevant statistics are difficult, if not impossible, to obtain, one has to resort to the more reliable figures for police deaths. Certainly there is clear evidence that a number of unarmed Metropolitan Police officers were shot at (and it must be remembered that only those serving in the outer divisions had the right to carry a firearm and then only at night).

The evident success of the London experiment led a number of other police forces to adopt similar policies

and some provincial policemen were still carrying a
revolver on night duty after the Great War while other
officers on special duties, such as Birmingham's
'Jewellery Patrol', were carrying guns in the inter-war
years. But the issuing of firearms remained the
exception rather than the rule, and when the Chief
Constable of East Sussex received a complaint in 1882
that one of his men was carrying a gun he ordered the
practice to cease forthwith.

The (limited) issue of revolvers to the Metropolitan
Police highlighted the anomaly of the seldom-if-ever
issued cutlasses, of which more than 5,000 were still
held in 1885. Most of these were deemed by the
Surveyor General of Ordnance to be useless and fit only
for scrap. The decision was taken to destroy all but 728,
those retained being held on the 20 divisions (ten each)
and by the detachments of the Metropolitan Police who
were responsible for the Naval Dockyards at Chatham,
Portsmouth, Devonport, Pembroke and at Woolwich.
These cutlasses were never officially withdrawn and
continued to be carried well into the twentieth century
by a few officers.

The Mounted Branch officers continued to carry a
sabre until 1925, when these were withdrawn and the
only weapon carried thereafter was the long, 'cavalry'
truncheon. Even this caused some concern and in 1931
a London newspaper referred to the Mounted Police
dispersing a demonstration by the use of swordsticks.
This brought a sharp rebuke from the periodical *Justice
of the Peace* which stated sternly that:

> London policemen do not carry swordsticks ... The
> mounted constable carries a long wooden truncheon,
> about the length of a sabre, furnished with a hand
> guard, but quite innocent of steel. It is a useful,
> efficient weapon but it is certainly not a swordstick.[26]

In 1909 a Metropolitan Police Board was given the

task of assessing 'whether the service revolver is suitable or should be replaced by some other type and whether the number allocated to each division is adequate'. After deliberation it came to the conclusion that the Webley revolvers supplied to the force should be replaced by Colt No. 3 automatic pistols. Other advice was sought and the Chief Inspector of Small Arms recommended the .32 Webley & Scott automatic pistol for general issue to police stations. Before any action was taken on these recommendations the infamous Siege of Sidney Street (of which more in the next chapter) took place, which highlighted the inadequacy of the Metropolitan Police's firearms.

The gathering of war clouds in 1914 brought a renewed emphasis to the question of arming the police. The Royal Mint was quick off the mark with a request that the police on duty there should be armed to prevent the ingress of foreign agents and saboteurs. The Commissioner agreed, adding a further threepence per weapon per day to the Royal Mint's private service agreement. This was followed by a general issue of firearms to police stations in London (and elsewhere) for use against any invading armies.

Following the Armistice in 1918, there was an upsurge of violent crime throughout the country, coupled with civil disorder and a resumption of Irish terrorist acts. Some sources suggest that the carnage on the Western Front had cheapened the value of human life. This predictably resulted in further press editorials, asking that 'something be done' and questions were asked in Parliament about providing the police with something more effective than a truncheon. This matter was referred by the Home Secretary to the Commissioner of the Metropolitan Police, General Macready, who minuted the file:

The Metropolitan Police are already supplied with

automatic pistols (.32) to the number of 1,006, which are distributed throughout divisions. These pistols are given to Police Officers who desire to have them when employed on night duty and who can, in the opinion of the Station Officers, be trusted to use them with discretion ... I think the Regulations in force for the carrying of pistols are sufficient, although, as I have said before, the numbers might with advantage be increased, together with the amount of ammunition allowed for practice.

In fact, the number of serviceable weapons held in the London divisions was much fewer than the Commissioner believed and there had been no training at all since it was suspended in 1915. However, the Home Secretary accepted the minute and later announced that '... no new departure is being made with regard to arming the Metropolitan Police ... For nearly forty years officers on night duty have been permitted, if they wish, to carry revolvers for their own protection.'

After the Great War, as a result of the activities mounted by Sinn Fein in connection with the Home Rule campaign, special patrols were instituted to protect vulnerable property, especially gunsmiths, and the officers detailed for this duty were all armed.

A survey carried out in 1926 revealed that there were 1,684 serviceable .32 pistols available in the Metropolitan Police (for a force of around 20,000, making the ratio less than one for every dozen officers). Ten years later there was a significant change in the instructions issued to members of the Metropolitan Police. The new Commissioner Sir Philip Game instructed that guns could no longer be drawn by a night-duty constable on request and that, in future, issues would be made only to those officers who could give a satisfactory reason for requiring them.

The outbreak of war in 1939, followed as it was by

the real possibility of invasion by the German Army, led to a radical rethinking of the position of the police *vis-à-vis* the carrying of firearms. A confidential letter from the Home Office in May 1940 stressed the non-combatant role of the police and stated that the carrying of arms for normal duties would be unnecessary or even undesirable. However, the letter went on to accept that there would be certain circumstance where the carrying of firearms would be justified, such as the guarding of vulnerable points against sabotage, protecting major police stations and the mounting of armed patrols of two to four men, especially in rural districts.

To meet these new threats, rifles were issued for probably the first time to the British police. These were mainly ancient Ross .303 weapons dating from the First World War but were deemed to be adequate for their purpose. By 1941 the Metropolitan Police had been issued with nearly 2,000 pistols (or about one for every ten officers) and it is interesting to note the distribution of these weapons. One had been lent to the Duke of Kent (who was later killed on active service with the RAF), 12 had been seconded to the aliens' detention camp on the Isle of Man, one was lost in a car crash and two were destroyed when Holloway police station was bombed. During that year a large number of American lease-lend revolvers were provided but these were regarded as being of 'doubtful quality'. In March 1942 all Metropolitan Police officers above the rank of Inspector were issued with a personal .45 revolver but these weapons were all withdrawn after the war.

The ending of hostilities in 1945 saw the anticipated increase in the number of ex-service weapons available to the ill-intentioned. Nearly every home had its souvenirs, including incendiary bombs (carefully polished!) and improperly retained service-issue weapons, ranging from the odd bayonet and SS dagger, through service revolvers to sub-machine guns. The opportunities for the criminal classes were immense and they lost no time in taking advantage of the situation.

Meanwhile, the availability of arms for the police appeared to be decreasing. When the Metropolitan Police's stock of .32 pistols was checked by the Inspectorate of Armaments in 1953, nearly 100 failed to fire and another 21 were considered likely to misfire. Fifty-four pistols were actually found to be unsafe and nearly 500 needed some form of repair or maintenance – a situation which was undoubtedly knowingly or unknowingly mirrored in many provincial forces. The Commissioner therefore sent a letter to the Home Secretary seeking authority for the purchase of 1,200 revolvers for general use and 50 Colt .38 automatics for the Special Branch and others engaged on security duties. The Receiver for the Metropolitan Police queried this application and suggested that revolvers could be supplied to the Special Branch men instead of pistols as he considered that revolvers could be carried in a shoulder holster with reasonable comfort. This suggestion was passed to one of the Assistant Commissioners who responded that he could

not agree that a revolver in a holster would be comfortable and inconspicuous when carried by a man wearing all forms of mufti. Special Branch, or officers on Royalty protection duty, have to look reasonably well-dressed. In well-fitting evening clothes it would be impossible to wear a revolver in a holster without it showing. In this country we do not like the thought of police being armed and we do not like the public to know that they are. Personally, I hate automatic pistols. I have had a good deal of experience with them in the Army and I look upon them as most dangerous ... All the same, I can see nothing for it but to have them for Special Branch and Royalty protection officers ...

This proposal was, in fact, adopted in 1953 and eventually Beretta self-loading pistols were purchased for use by the Special Branch while 750 Smith & Wesson .38 revolvers were bought from the Army for the rest of the force. These latter weapons were quickly discovered to be sub-standard. The War Office offered to replace them with surplus .38 Enfield revolvers but in the event were unable to muster sufficient of them and proposed to make .38 Webleys available instead. However, having been caught napping once, the Commissioner was not prepared to be caught again and insisted that all these weapons should be checked and tested before delivery. The results of these tests were such that negotiations with the War Office were broken off and eventually 500 new .38 Webley revolvers were purchased direct from the manufacturer: 'it would be quite improper to accuse the War Office of attempting to use the Metropolitan Police as a dumping ground for surplus arms in second-rate condition, but...'[27] The Berettas issued to the Special Branch and protection officers, being second-hand, also proved unreliable and in 1961 they were replaced with Walther 9mm pistols.

Soon afterwards the threat from terrorist organizations became acute and the question of arming at least some members of the police became much more urgent. Despite the considerable armoury now held by most police forces, especially the Metropolitan Police, the ordinary patrol officer was still unarmed. Following the pattern established over the years, from time to time there were calls in the press and in Parliament for the police to carry guns – usually after a policeman had been killed. One such incident occurred in 1966 when the three occupants of a police 'Q' car were shot down in cold blood by Harry Roberts, a former Army marksman who had seen service in Malaya. The event was described by the *Daily Mirror* in banner headlines as 'MASSACRED IN THE LINE OF DUTY' and the *Daily Mail* took up the cry, asking 'Is it time to give the policeman a gun?' The secretary of the Police Federation was quoted as saying, 'Either make a policeman's murder a hanging offence or give him arms to defend himself. Preferably the former.'

Information was received that Roberts was probably hiding in Epping Forest and the Metropolitan Police launched its biggest armed operation since 1911. But the hunt for the killer highlighted a number of shortcomings in relation to the arming of the police. One policeman, an authorized shot, had to ask for help with the loading of his revolver; his previous experience had been on Royalty protection when he used an automatic and he had never previously handled a revolver. In some stations there was found to be a dearth of revolvers; but this was nothing compared with the lack of authorized shots. At one station six revolvers were drawn from the armoury but only two of the officers being briefed were authorized to use them. Two other officers admitted to having had experience in the services and were duly issued with weapons, while the remaining two weapons were handed over to two other officers who said they were willing 'to have a go'. As one waiting officer was heard to remark, 'This is going to be the biggest balls-up since the seige of Sidney Street!'[28] Further 'organized chaos' was encountered at the scene of the manhunt, with at least one CID officer nonchalantly wandering around with a loaded and cocked revolver tucked into the waistband of his trousers. In the event, despite the massive hunt set up by the Metropolitan Police, Roberts was finally arrested by members of the much smaller Hertfordshire Police without a struggle or a shot being fired.

The Epping Forest débâcle demonstrated that the existing system of firearms training and authorization in the Metropolitan Police left much to be desired and a special Firearms Wing was formed, soon to be known as D11 and now referred to as SO19. Serving police officers with firearms experience gained in the armed forces were appointed as instructors after undergoing a course at the School of Infantry at Hythe (Kent). From dealing with two or three calls a year when it was first formed, the Metropolitan Police specialist firearms unit now deals with two or three calls *each day.*

When terrorists took over the Iranian Embassy in 1980, it was the SAS who eventually stormed the building and took the headlines. But it was the D11 snipers who spent many hours watching the windows through their telescopic sights, reporting every move made by the terrorists and made the final assault possible.

Four years later, when WPC Yvonne Fletcher was shot dead outside the Libyan People's Bureau, it was members of D11 who sat in the sewers beneath the building and passed back invaluable information about the occupants.

Following the Balcombe Street siege in December 1975 (of which more later), the public suddenly became aware that there were armed police on the streets of Great Britain. As Eldon Griffiths, MP, the Parliamentary consultant to the Police Federation at this time, pointed out:

> Balcombe Street revealed the extent to which our once unarmed police are now armed. But what the public as a whole has not appreciated is the sheer number and the growing normality of guns ... The number of guns now being carried and used by professional criminals and terrorists on the one hand and the policeman on the other is quite likely 100 times greater today than it was when we abolished the death penalty ...

Two decades later there is no indication that this escalation of the use of firearms has decreased – far from it. The continuing threat from terrorist organizations, coupled with armed robberies and the emergence of 'drugs barons', prepared to resort to lethal violence in order to protect their trade, resulted in firearms being issued to the police in London on no fewer than 5,968 occasions in 1980. The following year the number dropped to 4,983, while in 1982 the figure was estimated at around 5,800. During these three years firearms were only *used* by the police at six incidents in which three persons were wounded. However, the Stephen Waldorf affair in January 1983 (which is dealt with in more detail in the next chapter) aroused considerable alarm and the traditional, unarmed police officer was advocated by politicians and senior policemen as being both unique and beneficial to English society.

So far this chapter has tended to concentrate on the Metropolitan Police for the very good reason that, on the one hand, there is an understandable concentration of violent events in the capital and, on the other, the experience of that force, the largest by far in the country, is reflected to a lesser or greater extent in the provincial forces.

Without a significant Royalty protection role and a similarly reduced Special Branch commitment, provincial police tended to be armed only as and when a particular need was perceived. Following the recommendations of a working party set up by the Home Office after a number of unfortunate incidents in the early 1980s, each force created a specialist firearms team to be on call 24 hours a day. The declared intention was to have fewer but better trained police officers 'entrusted with arms'. Weapons were held at the more important police stations for issue on the instructions of an officer not below the rank of Assistant Chief Constable. Various incidents, not least of which was the Hungerford massacre in 1987, demonstrated that this system was inadequate to cope with most violent situations where time is of the essence and that needed to convey weapons from the police station to the site of an incident, especially in the larger rural forces, was completely disproportionate to the seriousness of the case.

The next stage, throughout the latter 1980s and into the 1990s, was to fit certain patrol cars, to be known as 'armed response vehicles' or ARVs, with a secure gun case in the boot in which a range of firearms could be held. These vehicles would be on permanent patrol and thus constantly available, although the authorization of a senior police officer was still needed before the weapons could be deployed. In London, these vehicles attend around 25 calls each day.

By this time the police had access to a wide range of weapons, ranging from the traditional handgun, through shotguns and sniper rifles to sub-machine guns. The last first made their public appearance in early 1986 when pictures appeared in the press showing officers openly carrying Heckler & Koch MP5 carbines. In fact, these particular weapons had been adapted to fire single shots only, although their considerable magazine capacity and accuracy were significant advantages over the handgun. The armed response vehicles also now carry a pair of these carbines, together with a Smith & Wesson model 10 .38 revolver for each officer and protective body armour and other special items of equipment.

In Kent, a fairly typical county police force, there were 76 incidents involving firearms in 1990 and armed response vehicles were quickly introduced, forming part of the Traffic Division. However, the growth in the number of calls for their involvement (there were around 160 firearms incidents in 1993 with a further, similar number of cases involving shotguns and knives) led to a discrete Central Firearms Unit being set up in 1994, consisting of highly trained firearms specialists (often ex-servicemen) to man the ARVs and also to provide VIP protection and weapons training for the rest of the force.

In May 1994, in response to the killing of Constable Patrick Dunne and Sergeant Derek Robertson and the shooting and wounding of two other officers in Brixton, the Commissioner gave his permission for Metropolitan officers crewing the armed response vehicles to carry the .38 revolvers on their belts and to use them at their own discretion. The Heckler & Koch carbines have still to be kept in the secure gun safe and may only be used with the express permission of an officer of at least Inspector rank (a considerable reduction from the original Assistant Chief Constable or Commander). To keep a sense of proportion it must be pointed out that these are specially trained officers and there were only 12 vehicles patrolling the whole of the capital. In fact, the total number of authorized firearms users in the Metropolitan Police in May 1994 was reported to be 1,888 out of a total strength of 28,000, or fewer than seven per cent.

There were inevitable criticisms of these proposals, the civil liberties group, Liberty, describing the move as 'dangerous and undemocratic'. 'The police are using the same tactics as the Government – they are dealing with the problems of crime rather than the causes. There is no evidence that people will be safer. More innocent people will be shot.'[29]

In response, the Commissioner, Sir Paul Condon, said,

I think we all value the traditional image of the British bobby. But we have to police the real world and the equipment and training must have some link with the real world. Having had two officers murdered, two shot and several stabbed, I am not prepared to ask my officers to carry out their duties without better protection.[30]

The Police Federation, representing the lower ranks of the police service, welcomed this initiative but felt that it had not gone far enough. The Federation was calling for officers in certain inner-city trouble spots to be armed as a matter of routine. In response to those who 'deplored the demise of Dixon of Dock Green', proponents of the policy of arming the police point out that, in the original film, *The Blue Lamp*, PC Dixon was shot dead by a criminal – something he might have avoided had he been armed. Mike Bennett, chairman of the Metropolitan Police Federation, said after the killing of Sergeant Robertson in 1994, that he had slowly come around to the view that the arming of officers as a matter of course was becoming an inevitable prospect. 'The people who are out there putting themselves at risk say they want to carry arms. We need to say "stuff the image" and make sure that our people are properly protected ... Firearms are the only sure defence.'[31]

At the Police Federation Conference in the summer of 1994, Fred Broughton, the chairman of the constables' central committee, told his members that additional protection was needed for the 'frontline constables':

> ... ARVs cannot protect officers who face armed confrontations on ordinary patrol. Many of these officers are patrolling areas of high crime and facing life-threatening confrontations. They receive a response time of between 30 and 60 minutes – it's unacceptable, it's totally inadequate.[32]

In fact, a Gallup poll carried out in the spring of 1994 revealed that 67 per cent of the general public felt that the police should be armed, whereas fewer than half the police officers polled wanted to be armed. It is of interest to note that, of the police officers voting, it was the rural officers who felt most at risk rather than those patrolling the violent inner city areas. The reason for this is undoubtedly because the city officer can quickly call for back-up while the rural man is much more on his own. Although most if not all forces have ARVs, the distances to be covered in rural areas in the larger counties mean that they cannot get to the scene of an incident as quickly as their urban colleagues.

There is a marked division of opinion among police officers as to the question of carrying arms, and what many police officers have in the back of their minds is the fact that, unlike a soldier in war, he or she will be personally responsible for the decision taken whether or not to use any weapon which may have been issued. The police officer will have to face the full enquiry which is launched every time a police bullet is fired, conducted by people who have probably never had to face the same dilemma and blessed with all the advantages of hindsight. The cases of Private Lee Clegg and Constable Patrick Hodgson quoted in the next chapter highlight this serious and fundamental problem.

There is little dissent, however, on the need to have better protection in the way of body armour and possibly some more effective weapon than the traditional truncheon. This is why more and more thought has been directed toward alternative types of police protection, such as side-handled batons, CS gas, pepper sprays or other non-lethal forms of restraint.

Although, as we have seen, the practice of policemen carrying firearms is not a new one, what has changed is its frequency and the overt way the weapons are carried. From the Heckler & Koch carbine-toting, anti-terrorist officers at airports, through the crews of ARVs, to officers on protection duties, the obvious visibility of weapons of all types has become almost commonplace. Photographs in the national press have shown uniformed policemen on duty outside 10 Downing Street with their pistols clearly visible, while others have depicted a Thames Valley Police officer cycling round the home of the Foreign Secretary with his Glock SLP high-capacity, automatic readily accessible at his belt.

But are these weapons just for show? In the next chapter we shall look at the occasions when a police officer has actually used his official weapon against a real or perceived threat to himself or others.

4 Deadly force

The exercise of police discretion is at its peak when the use of deadly force is contemplated, by whatever means this may be. The abolition of capital punishment in the United Kingdom, officially or in practice, occurred several decades ago and the decision by any police officer to take the life of another, no matter how serious or dreadful the offence which has been committed, is not one to be embarked upon lightly.

The circumstances of a particular case may, in the event, justify the taking of this extreme step but it is essential that this justification exists; without it the police officer may be guilty of manslaughter or even murder. A verdict of justifiable or excusable homicide will be returned only where the coroner's jury is convinced that there was no reasonable alternative to prevent another person from being killed and the doctrine of 'minimum force' has been applied.

In the United States the use of deadly force by a law-enforcement agent is seen by many commentators as 'execution without trial' and although no one was executed in that country in 1976, an estimated 533 persons were killed by police officers with legal justification and police action is by far the most frequent method by which the American government intentionally takes the lives of its own citizens.

What is exercising the minds of many thinking people is the possibility of this state of affairs arising or becoming more commonplace in Great Britain. As we saw in the last chapter, the British police are now more frequently bearing arms of one type or another and, consequently, one must expect the use of them to arise more frequently than in the past, where the circumstances justify such a course of action. So far as the legal position is concerned, the Criminal Law Act 1967 specified that 'A person may use such force as is reasonable', while Home Office guidelines stressed that firearms were to be used only as a last resort and that officers must always remember that responsibility for the use of the firearm is an *individual* decision which might have to be justified in legal proceedings.

As Sir Robert Mark, the then Commissioner of the Metropolitan Police stated in an address to Leicester University in 1976:

> A police officer armed in such circumstances will always be carefully briefed and, in a static situation, will be led by senior officers, but in the last resort it must be him and him alone who will decide whether he is justified in using his firearms ... A jury or police disciplinary inquiry may examine his action, but his use of a firearm does not differ in law from his use of a truncheon.

This question of being 'led by senior officers' means that these too must be properly trained in their responsibilities for the command and control of situations involving the use of police firearms. The first course of this type was organized by the West Yorkshire Police in the early 1970s and this initiative has since been followed by many other forces.

From time to time one hears critics suggesting that there is no need for the police to kill their targets and that they should 'shoot to wound'. Such suggestions reveal an astonishing degree of naïveté; once the police officer has taken the decision to fire, he or she knows that the result is likely to be the death of the target and will have taken this into account in deciding to fire. It must be assumed therefore that only in the most extreme circumstances will that decision have been taken and, once it has been, the objective must be to neutralize the target as quickly and efficiently as possible, bearing in mind that the life of the officer or a third party is genuinely seen to be at risk. If wounding the target would have the desired result (which, unless the wound is serious, is unlikely) then that is acceptable but, in the split seconds in which the action is taken, any deliberate attempt to wound would almost certainly be counterproductive and probably result in the death of the threatened person(s). Police officers, like their military colleagues, are taught to aim for the biggest target – the torso – which may or may not have the result of killing the target but will almost certainly have the desired effect of stopping him from carrying out the lethal threat which he is judged to pose.

Having made these points, let us not lose sight of the fact that the number of occasions on which the police in England and Wales (Northern Ireland is a special case) have opened fire is few. The first verifiable case of a Metropolitan policeman firing a revolver on duty occurred in 1887 when Constable Henry Owen fired six shots over the roof of a burning house in order to wake the occupants.

Twenty years later, two Russian anarchists, each armed with a handgun, attempted to rob a wages clerk in Tottenham. Although a number of shots were fired at the clerk and the driver of the car bringing him from the bank, neither was injured. A passer-by who attempted to 'have a go' was shot and wounded and the criminals were pursued by a rapidly growing posse of policemen and others. The fleeing robbers fired numerous shots at their pursuers, one of their bullets killing a ten-year-old boy, while one of the policemen borrowed a pistol from a bystander(!) and fired four shots in their direction, all of which missed. The chase continued and one policeman, Constable Tyler, who got too close for comfort was deliberately shot in the head and died shortly after admission to hospital. Two more of the pursuers were injured and another constable borrowed a pistol (they seem to have been freely available) and took some pot shots but he too missed. Unfortunately, in getting back from his firing position he was hit twice in the leg. Another constable used a borrowed revolver to shoot at the fugitives but missed. The two robbers then hi-jacked a tram and the three unfortunate passengers – an elderly man and a woman and child – were showered in glass as the crowd shot at the tram with shotguns and other weapons. When the tram had to slow down to allow an on-coming tram to pass, the woman and her child took the opportunity to get off but the male passenger was shot in the throat as he tried to follow them.

The incident then began to take on a Keystone Cops character. The pursuing police, now around 40 strong, stopped the passing tram and, ejecting the passengers, climbed aboard and sent the driver back the way he had come in pursuit of the robbers' tram. Meanwhile, another constable commandeered a pony-drawn cart and, carrying a service pistol, began to overtake this tram but the robbers fired and brought the pony down. The fugitives then dismounted because the tram was about to pass a police station and stole a milk cart instead, shooting the driver when he tried to stop them. When they crashed this they transferred to a greengrocer's cart, pursued by what was now a large crowd, mounted on carts, horses, motor cars – any form of transport at all. One constable was even to be seen riding a bicycle with a cutlass across the handlebars! A further attempt to stop the cart failed but resulted in its leaving the road where it was abandoned. One of the criminals, unable to climb the fence beside the river bank shot himself in the head and later died in hospital. The remaining ruffian shot another of his civilian pursuers and took shelter in a coal porter's house. From a first-floor window he kept up a barrage of shots until forced back by the heavy fire from his pursuers. One policeman, having borrowed a pistol from someone in the crowd, climbed a ladder and opened a back bedroom window. Meanwhile, two other officers, armed with service revolvers, broke into the house downstairs. The officer on the ladder got a glimpse of his quarry but was unable to operate the safety catch of his borrowed weapon and was saved from death by the fact that the Russian was nearly out of ammunition. He quickly slid down the ladder and joined the other two who had entered the ground floor, exchanging his defective pistol for one of the other officers' service revolvers. Taking the lead he mounted the stairs and called upon the robber to surrender and, getting no response, fired through the door panels, as did one of his colleagues. Another shot was heard and, when the party burst into the room, they found their quarry dead on the bed, having shot himself. The chase was over after the firing of around 400 rounds by the two murderers, killing two and injuring 25, some seriously.

The next significant occasion on which the police actually used firearms was probably the Sidney Street Siege of 1910, when an estimated 2,000 bullets were fired by the two sides, including military personnel. This incident began just before noon on Friday, 16 December 1910, when five City of London policemen were shot by armed burglars they had surprised at the back of a jeweller's shop in Houndsditch. Three of these officers died of their wounds while the other two were seriously injured. One of the perpetrators, who were again Russian nationals, was accidentally injured by his colleagues and the whole gang fled the scene, taking their wounded associate with them. Around 24 hours later, as a result of belated information from a doctor, the Metropolitan Police entered a house in the East End where they found the body of the injured Russian. In view of the fact that the original offence had occurred in the City of London police district and the criminals had gone to ground in the Metropolitan police district, the two forces collaborated closely and, although a number of arrests were made, three men remained at liberty: Fritz Svaars, Joseph Solokoff and Peter ('the Painter') Piaktow.

The trail led the investigators to a three-storey tenement building at 100 Sidney Street, Stepney, which was occupied by a number of Russian émigrés and, in the small hours of 3 January 1911, the City and Metropolitan forces each deployed 100 men in the area, cordoning off the surrounding streets. The innocent tenants and the landlady were evacuated into the cold January night, snow and sleet falling the whole time. The front door was left open and a gas lamp remained burning in the hallway. As the cold morning dawned, attempts were made to get the besieged killers to surrender but these were met with a fusillade of revolver shots, aimed at the police commanders who were crouching in a doorway opposite. A detective sergeant was wounded and the stretcher party evacuating him came under heavy fire, as did anyone else who dared show his face. The situation was summed up by Superintendent Mulvaney:

> It was palpable that these men dominated the situation, there was no approach to the house but by the front door, the roofs were of the kind known as gable and unapproachable. It was equally plain that any attack by the front door would have resulted in great sacrifice of life. Their weapons were far superior to our revolvers of which at this time we had only a few. It was therefore decided that Military Aid be sought as more effective weapons were required.[33]

Using their Mauser pistols the three killers went from room to room and from window to window, firing indiscriminately at anything which moved. With the arrival of reinforcements around 500 police were now on the scene and the crowd of onlookers grew by the minute. The Superintendent rode to the Tower of London and returned around 10.15 am with an officer, two NCOs and 17 volunteers from the Scots Guards. Taking up positions in nearby houses and making good use of their Lee Enfield rifles, the guardsmen drove the fugitives from their attic and second floor vantage points to the first and the ground floor where they were met with further rifle fire from other soldiers. Another 65 armed policemen arrived on the scene while other officers who had been sent to procure additional weapons began to arrive by taxi cab with a variety of pistols, shotguns and rook rifles which were quickly distributed to the more experienced officers. The Home Secretary Winston Churchill then arrived to take charge of the situation.

After around half an hour of fiercely exchanged fire, smoke was seen to be rising from the property, the occupants having started a fire hoping to make good their escape in the ensuing smoke and confusion. Shortly afterwards one of the killers was shot through the head as he tried to take aim at a target. The fire brigade duly appeared but, on the Home Secretary's orders, took no action. By this time a further military contingent of three officers and 51 other ranks had arrived, complete with a Maxim machine gun; a detachment of Royal Engineers came from Chatham and even a troop of the Royal Horse Artillery trotted up in the early afternoon. By this time the building was an inferno and the fire brigade was eventually permitted to try to control the flames still licking round the gutted building. Sadly, a collapsing wall buried five fireman, one of whom died from his injuries. As the building cooled a search was made of the smouldering ruin which revealed two charred corpses; none of the gunmen had survived the siege.

The incident revealed the sorry state of the weapons available to the police. The Metropolitan officers were using 30-year-old revolvers while the Adams revolvers used by their City colleagues had long been obsolete. Such rifles as were available to them consisted mainly of .22 target rifles and none of these weapons was a match for the awesome destructive power of the highly accurate, 7.63 Mauser pistol, two of which were found in the ruins, together with a 7.65 Browning. It is estimated that a thousand shots were fired by the police while the Army fired a further 500, against an estimated 500 fired by the besieged killers.

Not surprisingly the whole operation was severely criticized from several quarters and the recourse to the military questioned. But in fact the police were severely outgunned and had little option under the circumstances.

Further shoot-outs were extremely rare until after the Second World War when the proliferation of firearms encouraged criminals to go 'tooled up' when committing crimes. One of the more famous of such incidents took place in Croydon in 1952 when two men were seen to climb a gate into a warehouse one Sunday evening in November. Six local officers attended and one of them, Detective Constable Fairfax, climbed on to the roof where he saw both intruders hiding behind the top of the lift shaft. He called on them to come out but one of them suggested that the policeman come and get them. He did just that and grabbed hold of one of them, later identified as Derek Bentley who shouted, 'Let him have it, Chris!' It was later disputed whether this was an invitation to shoot or advice to surrender the weapon. Whatever the truth of the matter, the other man, Christopher Craig, fired his .455 Colt revolver with a sawn-off barrel and hit the detective in the shoulder. The injured officer managed to regain control of his prisoner and the other policemen arrived on the scene, led by Constable Sydney Miles. Craig fired again and Miles dropped dead with a bullet between the eyes. Further shots were fired and the unarmed policemen had to take cover until eight ancient Webley & Scott pistols were brought from Croydon police station. The injured Fairfax took possession of one of these and, with other armed officers, returned to the rooftop and called on Craig to surrender as he was now facing armed policemen. Fairfax fired two shots which were returned by Craig before the latter tried to escape by jumping off the roof. In doing so he fell 20 feet and fractured his spine.

Highly colourful and inaccurate reports appeared in the next day's press, telling of pitched gun battles with sub-machine guns, 200 police and a hand-to-hand battle on the rooftops. The tale was taken up again when Bentley, who was in custody when Constable Miles was killed, was hanged for murder, while his accomplice, who actually pulled the trigger and was too young to hang, was detained during Her Majesty's pleasure. Many theories and justifications have been advanced and many would agree that it was less than justice that Bentley should have paid the supreme penalty while his younger partner escaped the hangman's noose. It has even been suggested that Constable Miles was killed by a police bullet but this theory cannot hold water since the police weapons did not arrive on the scene until after his death.

Perhaps the reports of sub-machine guns having been used in the Craig and Bentley case were prompted by an incident which had occurred in Kent the previous year. During the night of 4 June 1951, some youths walking along a country lane in Luton, near Chatham, saw a masked man carrying a Sten gun which he pointed at them and then fired once. The youths ran for their lives and, about an hour later, reported the incident to Chatham police station. A sergeant and two constables drove to the scene in the station wireless van and, on arrival, the sergeant went with a witness to examine some sheds. One constable was left at the point where the gunman had last been seen while the other officer, Constable Baxter, remained with the van in radio contact with the force headquarters. None of these officers was armed. On reaching the sheds, the sergeant looked inside and saw the shadowy figures of a man and two women leaving it from the further end. He ran round to intercept them and, as he drew near, the man fired several single shots in his direction. The sergeant dived for cover while the two women ran off across the fields. Shots were then heard coming from the direction of the van and, hurrying to the spot, the sergeant found Constable Baxter lying in the road, mortally wounded. The wireless had been put out of action so the sergeant put his injured colleague in the van and drove to the nearest hospital where he later died.

At dawn the next morning a full-scale police operation to comb the area was mounted under the control of the Chief Constable Major John Ferguson, supplemented later by further police and military personnel. By this time the two women had been apprehended and were found to be absconders from an approved school. They confirmed the information already gathered by the police that the wanted man was Alan Derek Poole, a deserter from the Royal Signals and known to the police. A cordon was quickly thrown around his house in Symons Avenue, Chatham.

About 9 am there was a burst of fire directed at some officers covering the rear of the house. The fire was returned by the police and tear gas bombs were thrown into the house. At 10.45 am the Chief Constable ordered a direct assault on the house and Poole was found dead in an upstairs room with a loaded Sten gun across his body. A post-mortem examination revealed that Poole had taken a police bullet through the left shoulder which had penetrated his lungs. Death had followed shortly afterwards.

At the subsequent inquest it was held that Constable Baxter had been murdered by Poole and that Poole's death was justifiable homicide. It was never revealed which officer fired the fatal shot – it was probably never known.

These few incidents demonstrate that the police at that time (the immediate post-war period) were generally unarmed and that weapons were only issued when the occasion demanded. The exceptions were police officers engaged on specific protection duties, such as those responsible for guarding embassies and important personages. One such officer was Constable Slimon who, shortly after Christmas 1972, was returning to his post in Palace Green, Kensington where a number of foreign embassies were located. Like all such officers, Constable Slimon was armed that morning with a loaded .38 revolver. As he approached the corner of Kensington High Street and Campden Hill Road he heard an alarm sounding and was told that an armed hold-up was in progress at the bank on the corner. Drawing his revolver, the constable ran to the door of the building, calling out to the intruders that he was armed. One of the raiders immediately took aim with his sawn-off shotgun and fired at the same time as the officer fired his revolver. Both were wounded in the exchange, the constable being thrown back out of the doorway by the force of the shot. As he scrambled to his feet a number of bandits came out of the building, one of whom trained a revolver on the officer. Weak from loss of blood and in great pain, the constable managed to loose off one more shot which hit one of the raiders. The bank raiders drove off in a van which stopped a short distance from the bank to transfer the occupants and their loot into two other vehicles which awaited them. The arrival of a police dog-van caused them to abandon one of their wounded comrades in the street and, two hours later, the body of another robber was found – the first one shot by Constable Slimon – on the fifth floor of a multi-storey car park.

The incident provoked the expected and customary outcry. Members of Parliament raised questions in the House, demanding to know 'how many police are now carrying firearms ... how many police guarding embassies carry guns and what is the justification for it?' These, and other knee-jerk reactions, prompted the *Daily Telegraph* to publish a pragmatic leader in which it stated:

> The suggestion that he should have hurried to his post leaving the staff and customers of the National Westminster Bank to their fate or, alternatively, that he should have gone to the nearest telephone kiosk to get the approval of his superiors for intervention in the raid, is clearly absurd. It belongs to the realm of liberal fantasy.[34]

Once again the coroner's jury returned a verdict of justifiable homicide and Constable Slimon was rewarded with the George Medal.

Less than two months later another diplomatic incident took place which eclipsed the Kensington case. In February 1973, three young Pakistanis forced their way into the offices of the Indian High Commission in Aldwych. They were masked and armed with two revolvers, three knives, a sword and a spray of concentrated nitric acid and immediately took nine hostages. A window was smashed so that they could display these hostages to the authorities.

The first policemen to arrive at the scene were

unarmed and, threatened by the revolvers, withdrew to a safe distance. Two of the hostages took advantage of the confusion to jump through another plate-glass window and escape. The Special Patrol Group arrived, armed with revolvers and entered the reception hall from where they could hear the hostages pleading for mercy. One of the masked men pointed a handgun at the officers crying, 'I'll kill the lot of you!' while a second man, armed with both a gun and a knife ran to the terrified hostages and shouted, 'I will kill them. I will kill the bastards!' This second man was shot and killed by one of the officers while the other took cover behind a pillar, still pointing his gun at the police. Another armed officer made his way round the pillar and shot and hit the first man when it seemed that he was about to fire on him. The third (and youngest at 15) of the trio had by now been detained by other officers and his sword taken from him.

It was not until all three had been neutralized that the discovery was made that all the firearms were in fact good replicas of short barrelled Smith & Wessons. This fact not surprisingly gave rise to a great deal of controversy. Most of the newspapers for once gave a balanced account of the incident although the *Daily Telegraph* reported the Shadow Home Secretary Mrs Shirley Williams as saying that the police should be armed with weapons which fire rubber bullets and not lethal weapons and that organized crime and terrorism imported from abroad were eroding the 'gentlemen's agreement' between English petty criminals and the police not to carry firearms. No doubt the many police officers killed up to that date would have been more than a little interested in this 'gentlemen's agreement' which had so manifestly failed them in their hour of need. A suggestion by another commentator that the matter could have been resolved by the display of a little patience and negotiation obviously took no account whatsoever of the terror and real danger to which the unfortunate hostages were subjected, one of whom had already been injured in two places by sword cuts; one of which had fractured his skull.

The carrying of firearms by criminals is a serious and worrying trend which is only made worse by the use of imitation or replica firearms in robberies or hostage situations. So realistic are many of these replicas that it is impossible to tell them from the real thing other than by close inspection – something obviously denied those facing a brandished weapon, real or imitation. We have just seen how the weapons used in the occupation of the Indian High Commission were in fact excellent replica handguns, a fact which did not prevent those carrying them from being shot by the police.

A year after the Indian High Commission case there was another major incident which provoked banner headlines in much of the press. A little before 8 pm on Wednesday, 20 March 1974, Princess Anne, now the Princess Royal, was, with her then husband Captain Mark Phillips and a Lady in Waiting, being driven along the Mall towards Buckingham Palace. Her personal protection officer Inspector Beaton was sitting in the front next to the chauffeur. A white Ford Escort overtook them and then cut in in front of the Rolls-Royce and stopped. Thinking that this was an irate driver who believed he had been 'cut-up' by the Rolls, Inspector Beaton got out to attend to the matter. Because the Rolls had stopped close to the rear of the Escort, he had to walk round the back of the Royal car to reach the driver of the Escort. As he rounded the rear offside of the Rolls-Royce he realized that he was facing, not an irate driver, but an armed man holding a revolver. As the detective approached, the gunman fired three shots, one of which hit the officer in the shoulder. Beaton drew his Walther PPK 9mm pistol and fired at the gunman but missed. When he tried to loose off a second shot, the weapon jammed so he drew back behind the Rolls to try to clear the obstruction. Meanwhile the gunman, later identified as Ian Ball, tried to open the rear door of the Royal car, demanding that the Princess go with him. She and her husband struggled to keep the door closed while the Lady in Waiting escaped by the nearside door. The gunman told Beaton to drop his gun or he would shoot the Princess and, as he had been unable to clear the stoppage, the officer complied and got back into the car with the intention of trying to get between his charge and the assailant. Meanwhile, a journalist passing in a taxi, heard the sound of the shots and told the cabby to stop. He got out and walked back to the stationary Rolls-Royce where he had the temerity to simply ask Ball for his gun. Ball had, by this time, produced another revolver and with this shot the journalist in the chest and resumed his efforts to get into the Royal car. The occupants had now managed to close the rear offside door and Ball raised his weapon and threatened to shoot unless the door were opened. The Inspector put his arm in front of the Princess as Ball fired through the window, hitting the officer's right hand.

Another officer, Constable Hills, who was on duty nearby heard the sound of the shots and called for assistance on his personal radio before hurrying to the scene. Sizing up the situation he bravely approached Ball with the intention of disarming him but the latter shot him in the stomach at close range. Hills staggered to the rear of the Rolls-Royce where he used his radio to call for urgent assistance and, seeing the pistol which Beaton had dropped earlier, picked it up with the intention of using it against the would-be kidnapper. He was too weak from his wound, however, and collapsed in the roadway. With all external resistance removed, Ball pulled open the rear door of the Rolls and deliberately shot Beaton in the stomach. The unfortunate officer, who had now been wounded three times and was bleeding profusely both externally and internally, fell out of the car and lay in the roadway. At some time during the affray the chauffeur of the Royal car had been shot in the chest and he too was out of action.

Another chauffeur who saw what was going on pulled his Jaguar across in front of Ball's Ford to prevent its escape. He got out and went up to Ball who, for some reason, refrained from shooting the new arrival and merely stuck a gun in his ribs and told him to clear off. The chauffeur wisely obeyed but left his car where it was and went to assist the wounded constable. Another taxi passenger arrived on the scene and tried to hit Ball as he was attempting to drag the Princess from the car. Ball fired at him but missed and there followed a struggle during which several police cars arrived on the scene. With the arrival of these reinforcements, Ball ran off but was brought down by a classic rugby tackle by one of the newly-arrived officers. In his pockets were found a ransom note for £3,000,000 and a free pardon in respect of all crimes committed during the kidnap attempt. He also had the two revolvers and four pairs of handcuffs.

In due course Ball was found guilty on two counts of attempted murder, two counts of wounding with intent and one of attempted kidnapping. He was detained under the provisions of the Mental Health Act. The courageous Inspector Beaton was awarded the George Cross while Constable Hills and the second taxi passenger each received the George Medal. The driver of the Royal car and the journalist were both awarded the Queen's Gallantry Medal.

In the summer of 1975, Home Office approval was sought for the formation in London of four special firearms teams, composed entirely of volunteer instructors, to deal with incidents of serious armed crime or terrorist activity. Although the SAS would be called in where terrorists were concerned, there would necessarily be some delay before these élite forces could arrive on the scene and there was seen to be a pressing need for highly trained police officers to contain a particularly serious incident pending their arrival. These officers would be equipped with pump-action shotguns, CS gas cartridges and body armour. While the bureaucrats were still debating the proposal, a further serious incident occurred which gave these provisionally formed teams a chance to try out their skills.

In the early hours of Sunday, 28 September, staff from several branches of the Spaghetti House restaurant chain gathered together at the headquarters of the firm in Knightsbridge to check and pay in the weekend's takings – a sum of around £13,000. This money was packed into two briefcases carried by the general manager and a director of the company, and the nine members of staff, all Italians, prepared to leave. As they reached the front door, three armed men entered from the street and demanded the cash. One was waving a sawn-off, double-barrelled shotgun while the other two brandished handguns. Taking advantage of the dim lighting, the two men carrying the cases slid them under some tables, out of sight. The Italians were all shepherded downstairs to the basement but the general manager managed to escape and raised the alarm. The police arrived on the scene and cautiously entered the ground floor. Hearing the footsteps above them, the robbers led their charges into a basement storeroom and told the police to keep away or they would shoot. The robbery had thus become a siege and the victims had become hostages.

The area round the restaurant was contained and the wild demands made by the gunmen for the release of black prisoners, the attendance of the Home Secretary and the placing of an aircraft at their disposal were all brusquely rejected. The only concession was the provision of a radio and the offenders were left in no doubt that the only way they would leave the premises would be as prisoners.

The radio provided a means of communication between the besieging police and the besieged criminals while a visual probe had been inserted into the storeroom which gave the police controller a view of the interior. At one point a shot was heard but, thanks to the probe, the controller was able to confirm that this was an accident – a fortunate state of affairs since, otherwise, the police might well have stormed the room, believing that the occupants were in mortal danger.

Despite the attendance of a number of important diplomatic personages, the siege reached a stalemate. Any attack on the storeroom had to be discounted because of the danger to the remaining hostages (two had already been released) and the declared objective was to arrest the gunmen without incurring any casualties among the hostages or the police. By the Thursday the gunmen were getting irritable and the strain was beginning to show. This was aggravated the next day when the light in the storeroom was switched off for the first time. After heated discussion among themselves, the gunmen announced that they were releasing the prisoners and the six unharmed Italians thankfully emerged from the storeroom. Two of the gunmen also announced that they wished to come out but, before they did so, a gunshot was heard. The shotgun and a handgun were then pushed out of the storeroom in token of surrender and the two gunmen followed. The third man, the leader, was found with a self-inflicted gunshot wound in the stomach, lying on the floor of the storeroom. On this occasion, despite the impressive array of arms available to the police and the excellent training opportunity it provided, the incident was resolved without a single shot being fired by the police – a stark contrast to the Sidney Street siege, for example.

Apart from ordinary criminals, the activities of terrorist groups was a continuing cause for concern throughout the last third of the twentieth century. In particular, the IRA, the direct descendants of the Fenian groups of the previous century, posed a constant threat to law and order on mainland Britain. One incident involving members of this terrorist organization resulted in yet another siege.

Only a few days after the Spaghetti House siege four men in a stolen car raked the front of Scott's Restaurant in Mayfair with machine guns. The alarm was raised and two police officers on foot spotted the stolen car in Portman Square. They grabbed a taxi and gave chase until the stolen car came to a halt in a close. The four occupants got out and ran off, firing handguns at the two unarmed policemen who were similarly now on foot. By now two Special Patrol Group personnel carriers had arrived and, as one pulled in front of the fleeing men, another came alongside them and stopped to allow the occupants to get out. As they did so, they were fired on by the gunmen, fortunately without their hitting anyone. Two of the Special Patrol Group officers used their service revolvers to return the fire but they too missed. The gunmen now turned tail and ran back the way they had come, towards their original, unarmed pursuers who took shelter in a doorway. The arrival of an unmarked Flying Squad car caused the fleeing men to scatter and they were lost sight of in Balcombe Street.

When the police officers arrived they were told that four men had just run into the basement to some council flats. The area was cordoned off and armed police were posted outside. A thorough search was made of the basement area and it was eventually determined that the gunmen had taken refuge in the first floor flat of a Mr and Mrs Matthews who were being held hostage. The well-oiled siege machinery, honed at the Spaghetti House incident only a few days earlier, was brought into action. On this occasion, since it was fairly clear that terrorists were involved, the Special Air Service was called in and arrived in the early hours of the next day. Sandbagged sniper emplacements were set up overlooking the rear of the building and on the front landing facing the door to the flat where no other cover was available.

This public appearance of the D11 firearms specialists really brought their existence to the notice of the press and the public for the first time. The *Daily Mail*, which carried photographs of the sandbag emplacements being erected (together with a completely erroneous artist's impression of one of these specially-trained policemen) commented:

> The fact that the siege has made the public realize London has this élite force of professional marksmen ready to kill or maim if necessary is bound to raise the question: 'Are we moving too quickly towards other countries which have permanent para-military police units?' Strength could be added to the argument because the marksmen ... were themselves allowed to choose their own paramilitary uniform, choose and get the guns they want, and are completely in control of training methods.[35]

Happily, the hostages were released after nearly six days of captivity which they had borne with great fortitude and, shortly afterwards, the terrorists themselves came out with their hands up. Subsequently a Sten gun, an Armalite rifle, two .30 carbines, three .357 revolvers, two .38 Colt revolvers and two other pistols were recovered – an indication of the impressive firepower available to the terrorists, who were all sentenced in due course to life imprisonment for a series of terrorist activities, including murder.

Once again the actual siege was resolved without a shot being fired by the forces of law and order, but there is no doubt that it was the immediate availability of a range of weapons and of highly trained men willing to use them which ultimately led to the surrender of these desperate men. As Eldon Griffiths, the parliamentary consultant to the Police Federation, stated in an article in the *Daily Telegraph*:

> Balcombe Street revealed the extent to which our once unarmed police are now armed. But what the public as a whole has not appreciated is the sheer number and growing normality of guns ... The number of guns now being carried and used by professional criminals and terrorists on the one hand and policemen on the other is quite likely 100 times greater today than it was when we abolished the death penalty[36]

As if terrorist activity were not enough, the 1970s saw a spate of armed robberies in London and other cities. A fairly typical example occurred in Eltham, in south London, towards the end of 1978 where, as a result of a number of armed robberies, unmarked police cars were patrolling the area on robbery patrol.

One late December afternoon, one of these cars, containing three armed, plain-clothes detectives, was keeping a casual eye on a Securicor van outside a supermarket from where the three-man crew were collecting cash, when a stolen car drew alongside the Securicor vehicle and two men carrying sawn-off shotguns leapt out and attacked one of the security men. Two of the policemen immediately got out of their 'Q' car and ran to the scene, shouting to the robbers that they were armed and telling them to drop their guns. Instead, one of the robbers turned his attention to the approaching policemen and trained his shotgun on them. One of the policeman fired two unaimed shots at the robber but missed and, with the stolen car beginning to move off, the robber aimed his gun in the direction of the detective and a Securicor guard. The same policeman, a detective sergeant, fired another two shots, one of which hit the bandit and his accomplices promptly drove off at speed, leaving their wounded colleague lying in the road. The wounded criminal was taken to hospital where he died shortly afterwards from a gunshot wound. His shotgun was recovered and both barrels were found to be loaded and one of the hammers cocked. The dead man had several convictions, including two for armed robbery and, at the subsequent coroner's inquest, the jury found that the killing had been justifiable homicide.

Perhaps the worst period so far in the history of the British police, so far as weapons are concerned, occurred early in 1983 with what has become known as the Waldorf affair. The story began with the hunt for one David Martin, a peculiar but vicious 35-year-old criminal who had a propensity for carrying out armed robberies while dressed in women's clothes. He was apprehended in August 1982 but escaped by shooting his way out, seriously injuring a constable in the process. A month later he was picked up in the street, wearing his favourite disguise, and produced two loaded handguns which he would undoubtedly have used had he not been stopped by a bullet in the neck, fired by one of the police officers. When he had recovered from his wound in hospital, he was charged with attempted murder, armed robbery and a number of burglaries, one of which was at a gunsmith's where a number of weapons had been stolen, several of which had not been recovered.

While detained in the cells at Marlborough Street Magistrates' Court Martin managed to escape on Christmas Eve. Given his record and the fact that he was believed still to have access to a number of firearms, a special task force was set up with the specific role of recapturing this highly dangerous criminal. One section of this special squad kept watch on the Hampstead flat of a girl friend of Martin's, Susan Stephens, and followed her movements in the hope that Martin would make contact. One evening in the middle of January 1983, a series of unmarked police cars were following and keeping watch on a hired Mini in which Miss Stephens was a back-seat passenger. The car was being driven by Lester Purdy and the man in the front passenger seat was Stephen Waldorf who, unfortunately, bore more than a passing resemblance to Martin. As the evening wore on the following police teams became more and more confident that they were indeed following this dangerous criminal and his friends.

At one point near Earls Court the traffic had slowed sufficiently for one of the detectives to alight and walk along the pavement towards the suspect car. This officer was, in fact, the only one of the followers who actually knew Martin, having been among those who had arrested him earlier. He equally knew that Martin would be able to recognize him and would undoubtedly react violently if he were seen. With only the light of the street lamps to assist him in his identification of this passenger in a darkened car and, given his understandably jumpy state of nerves, the officer wrongly identified the Mini's passenger as the wanted man. He had drawn his revolver and, when this passenger reached into a bag on the back seat, he suspected the worst and fired twice, first at the car's tyre and then at the man he was convinced was Martin. Another officer, hearing the shots, thought his colleague was under attack and fired at the car. A total of 14 shots were loosed off before the terrible mistake was realized. Fortunately, Waldorf recovered from his wounds and was later awarded a considerable sum as damages against the police. The two officers who had fired on the vehicle were both charged with attempted murder and other offences but were acquitted. This terrible tragedy continues to be cited by opponents whenever the question of arming the police is raised.

Another shooting incident occurred later the same year when an attempt was made to assassinate the Israeli Ambassador by a fanatical Jordanian. The would-be assassin was chased by the Ambassador's Special Branch bodyguard and, when he turned to fire on his follower, the officer opened fire and injured him. When the Jordanian eventually came before the courts charged with attempted murder his counsel suggested that the officer's life was never in danger and submitted that the officer acted incorrectly in shooting him. However, in his summing up, the judge, Mr Justice Mars-Jones, quickly dispelled this contention:

> It would be unlawful for a police officer to shoot a suspect to prevent him from escaping but, in this case, there is no doubt that Detective Constable Simpson saw his charge being shot in the head at close range. When the Ambassador fell he chased the gunman up Park Lane while he was still carrying a gun. Then, in South Street, he called on the person he believed to be the gunman to stop – and he failed to do so. The law is not so stupid as to forbid a police officer in such circumstances to resort to the ultimate remedy of shooting a gunman, and whose failure to do so would allow an armed man who had demonstrated he had a killer instinct to escape with a machine-pistol and to allow the same man to do the same thing again.

Towards the end of 1991, a man was seen with a handgun in the centre of Wellington, Shropshire and a number of armed police officers were deployed with a view to apprehending him. The man, later identified as Ian Gordon, aged 24, who had a known history of mental illness, was located by Inspector Alan Barrell and Sergeant Graham Cooke of the West Mercia Police. Despite their repeated pleas, Gordon refused to put down his weapon and threatened to shoot the officers. Moments later, Gordon raised his pistol and pointed it at the Sergeant saying, 'You're dead!' The two officers immediately opened fire, killing the suspect. It was subsequently discovered that the weapon concerned was a defective air pistol but closely resembled a 9-mm semi-automatic. The officers stated at the inquest that they were convinced they were dealing with a dangerous man, armed with a real and deadly weapon. The coroner's jury returned a verdict of lawful killing after a hearing which lasted 15 days and involved evidence from 55 witnesses.

Around the same time another gunman was shot dead on the other side of the country. Early in 1992 police attended a domestic incident in a house in Bury St. Edmunds, Suffolk, where Barry Clutterham, aged 47, was involved in the latest round of a long-standing dispute with another man. As the officers were about to speak to him, Clutterham produced a sawn-off shotgun and smashed the nearside passenger window of the police car. He then fired at point-blank range at Constable Keith Bottomly who, fortunately, was only injured. Clutterham then hijacked a learner's car, taking the instructor hostage, and was pursued by the police. The car was eventually stopped in a nearby village and Clutterham got out, still with his weapon. After being challenged and refusing to lay down the weapon, Clutterham was shot and killed by two police officers.

Since then there have been a number of cases where criminals have been shot by police officers in the course of carrying out some criminal activity or because they were peceived as being armed and dangerous.

In September 1992 a suspected armed robber was shot in a police ambush outside a bank in Hackney, east London and a police officer was also shot. The next month the police in Heathfield, East Sussex shot a man after a three-hour hostage drama involving the gunman's estranged wife, during which the offender had opened fire with two shotguns.

In February 1993, a man, bizarrely wearing a toy police helmet, was shot in the chest during a police ambush in Crouch End, north London. In May the same year, the police in Strathclyde shot and wounded a man after several police and motorists had been injured by him. At the other end of the country, the police near Dover, Kent shot a man in the stomach in July 1993. He had been running amok with a double-barrelled shotgun and had fired six times at the officers before he was himself shot.

In October 1993, the armed robber David Stone was shot in the back of the head and killed after the police cornered him in Holloway, north London after a bank raid. Also in Holloway, in July 1994, John O'Brien was shot by the police following a siege and died in hospital.

Ian Fitzgerald-Hay, a farmer, was shot and killed near Totnes, Devon after firing on a police dog and taking aim at police officers while, again in London (Enfield), a 30-year-old man was shot and critically injured after shooting a policewoman in the leg. Less than 24 hours after the last incident, Robert Dixon was shot dead in West Yorkshire. This case is looked at in more detail in the next chapter.

The cases described in this chapter are mere illustrations of the types of occasion where the police, who over the years have been issued with firearms for special duties, have actually had to open fire. The incidents cited are not exhaustive and, although most of these occurred in the capital, a number of similar events have taken place in the provinces in the last century or so. However, it is to be expected that, given the concentration of diplomatic and financial institutions in London, the majority of cases of serious armed robbery or attempted assassination will take place there and, consequently, most calls on the armed British police occur in and around the capital. For example, although the West Mercia Police were called to deal with 31 incidents involving firearms in 1991, 12 of which concerned direct confrontation with armed offenders, members of that force have only once discharged firearms in more than ten years.

At this point, and before leaving the subject of the police use of firearms in the United Kingdom, special mention should be made of Northern Ireland. Throughout the centuries, going back some 800 years, there has been conflict in or concerning Ireland. We have seen how the Fenians were struggling violently for independence from British rule in the nineteenth century and the campaign for Irish independence was much on the mind of the British government when, in the early part of the nineteenth century, it formed a police force which became known as the Irish Constabulary, later granted the prefix 'Royal'.

The Royal Irish Constabulary was an efficient paramilitary force which formed the model for many subsequent colonial police forces. Its members were armed and drilled in a military manner and it successfully policed the whole of Ireland until partition in 1922 when the south became the independent Irish Free State. This division of Ireland resulted in the disbanding of the Royal Irish Constabulary which had been involved in many a violent and armed skirmish in its one hundred years' existence.

A new police force was formed in the south, the *Garda Siochana*, and what is now the Republic of Ireland ceases to be of direct interest to us as it no longer forms part of the United Kingdom.

But the northern part of that troubled island remained, and still remains, part of the United Kingdom of Great Britain and Northern Ireland. Policing the six counties of Northern Ireland is entrusted to the Royal Ulster Constabulary which took over from the Royal Irish Constabulary in 1922 when that body was disbanded.

If the politicians had hoped that the partition of Ireland would lead to peace they were sorely disappointed. There remained a strong body of opinion in the south that the whole of Ireland should be re-united and this point of view is supported by a significant minority in the north. Nevertheless, the majority of the population in Northern Ireland are vehemently opposed to any idea of unification and successive British governments have supported the wish of the Ulstermen to remain part of the United Kingdom.

Over the years this fundamental difference of opinion has led to many a violent outbreak of disorder and, in 1968, the Irish Republican Army – the IRA – began a concerted campaign of violence in an effort to make the British government change its mind. This campaign lasted for a quarter of a century and, at the time of writing, there exists a fragile peace in Ireland.

All of this had, of course, a significant effect on the policing of Northern Ireland. Although the RUC quickly moved away from the paramilitary nature of its predecessor and became basically an unarmed force, the disorders and concerted violence of the last 25 years meant that personal weapons had to be reissued and recourse made to the British Army for assistance – something not seen on mainland Britain for very many years.

But, although there exists an armed police force in the United Kingdom, it must be borne in mind that the weapons are issued to combat terrorist attacks and not ordinary crime. The occasions on which members of the RUC have opened fire have almost invariably been when they believed that the targets were involved in some form of terrorist activity, and the same applies to the troops who are there in support of the civil power.

It is therefore of interest to consider the case of Private Lee Clegg of the Parachute Regiment. While assisting the police in their counter-terrorist role, Private Clegg and other soldiers were manning a road block when a car approached at speed and gave a clear indication that it was not going to stop. Fearing a terrorist attack, Private Clegg opened fire on the approaching vehicle. It was later alleged that, although two shot were fired as the vehicle approached and while it still represented a potential threat, a third shot was fired after the vehicle had passed. This shot killed Karen Reilly, a passenger in the vehicle, which was, in fact, a stolen car with no terrorist connections. Private Clegg was charged with murder in July 1991. At his trial it was held that the third bullet was not fired in self-defence as the vehicle had already passed, taking with it the imminent threat. The court ruled that Private Clegg was not justified in firing this shot and, in June 1993, he was convicted of the murder of Karen Reilly.

Although this was a soldier, the position would have been exactly the same had the shots been fired by a policeman, as they could quite well have been. Although Clegg was later released from prison on the grounds that exceptional circumstances surrounded this case, it is salutary to note that the forces of law and order are not themselves above the law and, should a police officer kill or injure someone without justification, he or she will face the full rigours of the law. This is clearly demonstrated in the more recent case involving Constable Patrick Hodgson, which we shall be examining later.

5 To be, or not to be …

To be, or not to be, armed, that is the question. Unlike Hamlet, the British police do not merely have to suffer the slings and arrows of outrageous fortune but the knives, shotguns and revolvers of violent and desperate criminals. So, should they bear arms as a matter of course, as is the custom in most other countries? There are many varied and cogent arguments both in support of and against the idea, even within the police service itself.

Michael Shersby, MP, the current parliamentary adviser to the Police Federation is of the opinion that: 'the number of officers who ask to carry firearms routinely is very small. Most officers definitely do not wish to be armed.'[37] In support of this contention Mr Shersby quotes a survey carried out by the Federation among members of the Essex force in the spring of 1991, to which 2,200 of the total establishment of 2,800 responded. Of these an overwhelming 77 per cent were opposed to the idea of routinely carrying firearms. This point of view was reinforced by the members of the Association of Chief Police Officers who, three years later, decided that they were opposed to routine arming, with the caveat that they nevertheless shared the view of the lower ranks that the day was approaching when such a step might be inevitable.

However, contrary to the views expressed by the Police Federation's parliamentary adviser and to the findings of the admittedly small-scale survey carried out in just one of the forty-odd forces in the country, a comprehensive poll conducted by the Federation in

1994 revealed that no fewer than 45 per cent of the lower ranks felt that they needed the protection of a firearm to perform their duties effectively.[38]

It would therefore be fair to say that, of those police officers 'at the sharp end', nearly half currently wish to be issued with guns and that, based on earlier surveys, this number is growing rapidly. The reason for this is not hard to find; there is a growing perception that contemporary society is a violent one and that the representatives of law and order are among those most at risk. In previous chapters we examined this phenomenon and, while one would not wish to become involved in a detailed analysis of statistics and all that that involves, one simple example may serve to illustrate the trends.

The first report of the Chief Constable of the Tunbridge Wells Borough Police in 1892 referred to 23 arrests and 12 people being committed for trial (for indictable offences); in 1992, a hundred years later, for the same area, there were 3,144 arrests and 1,859 committals. In other words, there were 137 times as many arrests and 155 times as many committals in 1992 as in 1892. So far as burglary and housebreaking were concerned, the Victorian police force recorded a mere five cases against a total of over 1,500 a century later! However, cases of murder and manslaughter remained surprisingly similar: two in 1892 and three in 1992.

These figures tend to suggest that, while crime overall has risen to an extraordinary extent over the century, violence has not really increased at all. This is supported by the particularly interesting revelation that assaults on the police in the earlier year totalled 12 whereas the 1992 figure was 20 – an insignificant increase. The fact that cases of drunkenness in the last century were some 50 per cent greater than in the recent past (128:83) indicates perhaps that the average Victorian was more prone to get drunk and was more ready to resort to fisticuffs than Englishmen nowadays. Of course, the police establishments have increased over the years but to nothing like the extent to which offences have risen; a total of 41 men in the old Borough force (including the Chief Constable) had grown to 142 all ranks in the equivalent police sub-division of the County force. This example is not, of course, necessarily representative of all parts of the country but it does give an indication of how certain crime trends have developed in the past century or so.

Are the police more at risk of being killed (and by extension, of being seriously injured) today than they were in the past? As the statistics set out in Table 1 (see Ch. 2) demonstrate, the number of police officers killed in Victorian Britain averaged around two each year, a figure which fell to only half this number in the twentieth century. Not until the 1960s and the 1970s did the number rise once more to about 1.5 per annum and it was not until the 1980s with an average of 2.5, that the mortality rate reached a level slightly higher than that during most of the previous century. In fact, the police death rate in the 1870s was marginally higher than that for the 1980s (26 against 25). So far as the current decade is concerned, it is too early to make any judgement, the figures for the four years 1991–94 being, respectively, four, one, two and two.

How do these facts support the perception that there is an increased propensity on the part of even petty criminals to use weapons (not necessarily firearms) against the police? It is probably impossible to obtain any reliable statistics since the parameters are unclear. Are we talking about mere threats and the brandishing of a weapon of some sort (and what is a weapon?) or actual woundings and, if the latter, should we consider mere scratches or only life-threatening injuries?

In the absence of statistical evidence we have to resort again to the more reliable figure for deaths through criminal violence (although even this is not entirely helpful since medical advances may have saved the lives of some officers who, a century earlier, would surely have died). What is clear is the fact that the use of firearms against the police has grown over the years. In the last century firearms accounted for about a quarter of the police deaths whereas more recently the proportion has been a half or even more.

All of which brings us to question whether the routine arming of the police would (a) reduce crimes of violence and (b) better protect officers. It must be said that there is little evidence to support any contention that an armed police force reduces the levels of violence generally. Would the average bank robber leave his sawn-off shotgun at home if he thought that the police called to the scene would be armed? Probably not, since the shotgun is used primarily to intimidate the bank staff and the robber has no thought of getting involved in a shoot-out with the police. Since the threat of violence is an essential element in armed robberies, only the presence of armed guards at the target premises is likely to have any deterrent effect.

As for better protecting the police themselves, this is an entirely different matter. Since the use of a firearm against, say, a knife-wielding criminal is likely to be discouraged except in the most exceptional circumstances (such as where the life of another person is clearly at risk), we come back to the scenario where the policeman is confronted by a criminal brandishing a firearm with the evident intention of using it either to pursue his illegal intention or to evade arrest. Once again the question of life-threatening circumstances arises and this is most likely to be present where the criminal is trying to evade capture by a policeman who has been called to the scene or has stumbled across the incident. There seems little doubt that, as in the case when Constable Slimon shot a fleeing bank robber who threatened him with a shotgun (see Ch. 4), when the police officer arrives on the scene with the knowledge that a crime is in progress, he will be in a better position to arrest the perpetrators without undue risk to himself if he is already armed. He will have drawn his weapon and will approach the scene with a degree of circumspection.

It is where a police officer stumbles across an incident by accident, such as when Constable Patrick Dunne unexpectedly came upon some drug traffickers who did not hesitate to shoot him dead, that the value of the police firearm is less clear. It would certainly call for very quick reactions, since the criminal is more likely to have his weapon ready to use and be prepared to shoot and ask questions afterwards (if at all) than the policeman who knows he will have to justify his actions to armchair critics later. The debate as to whether, in the case quoted, the constable would have been able to defend himself against his murderers had he been carrying a gun, is likely to continue well into the future. In fact we shall never know, although the indications are that, in this particular case, by the time the constable had sized up the situation and drawn his weapon, he would already have been rendered *hors de combat* by his killers.

To summarize, then, where a police officer is called to an incident, especially one where he or she is aware that firearms are being used or are likely to be used, if the officer is armed, he or she will have a better chance of either detaining or, in extreme circumstances, neutralizing (to use an Americanism) his quarry. In addition, if firearms are used against the officer, as a threat or by actual discharge, in the course of the crime or during any subsequent pursuit, that officer will have a chance of getting his or her shot in first, thereby both ensuring a measure of self-protection and the possibility of stopping the criminal.

A detailed examination of every case in which a police officer was killed would give an indication as to whether that particular incident would have been prevented had the officer been armed. But every incident is different and, even if one could say that the majority of these officers would have had a chance of surviving had they been armed (an unlikely outcome), this would provide no guarantees for the future.

One area which is often overlooked is the use of firearms to destroy injured or crazed animals, but this represents a large proportion of the uses in some countries. For example, in the Rheinland-Pfalz province of Germany, an average of 275 shots were fired at animals ('dangerous, sick or other animals') in each of the years from 1989 to 1993, against just six each year aimed at persons. This sort of use must, of course, be regarded as a side issue, but a police officer who has to deal with a road accident in which an animal has been gravely injured would probably welcome the availability of some means of putting the animal out of its misery without the painful and clearly fruitless delay involved in getting veterinary attention. There is also the possibility of wild or berserk animals presenting a serious danger to the public. These might be carnivorous animals which had escaped from a zoo or cattle absconding from an abattoir, although it must be admitted that, in such circumstances, the sort of handgun issued to patrol officers would probably be inadequate unless used with great accuracy and from close range. Nevertheless, this possibility must be seen as a further (albeit peripheral) argument in favour of arming the police.

These, then, are some of the arguments in favour of routinely arming the police in Great Britain. But what of the other side of the coin? The British police have always been proud of the fact that they are an unarmed service, unlike most of their foreign counterparts (although, as we have seen, this is not strictly the case). Yet the fact remains that, as a general rule, the police in this country do not routinely carry a firearm and, after more than a century and a half, the arguments for changing the status quo must be convincing indeed if any change is to be seriously contemplated.

Opponents of the idea of routinely arming the police point out that the use of firearms by criminals in this country is still, fortunately, rare. Research carried out in the Metropolitan Police District by the Oxford University Centre for Criminological Research showed that in the 1,100 cases of serious armed robbery examined firearms were discharged in only four per cent of them. In nine cases out of ten where shots were fired there were no physical injuries. This means that, on average throughout 1990, in only one serious armed robbery out of 200 was anyone injured.[39] There would certainly seem to be evidence that the use of both firearms and other lethal weapons, especially knives, is growing, but it must be questioned whether this growth is yet sufficient and the numbers adequate to justify such a fundamental change in the concept of British policing.

It may also be said that the arming of the police would bring a threefold risk in its wake. First, the fact that the police are known to be armed would be a further incentive for criminals to carry such weapons themselves; secondly, innocent bystanders would be at risk from shoot-outs between the police and armed desperadoes; thirdly, there would be an increased danger of innocent persons being shot, as in the Waldorf case we examined earlier.

The first contention is supported by Michael Shersby, MP, who has stated that:

... I do believe that to arm them [the police] would play into the hands of the violent minority of

> criminals that carry arms. It would escalate the use of
> guns on criminal escapades. Gone, unfortunately, are
> the days when criminals would 'frisk' each other
> before going off to do a 'job'. They were deterred by
> the thought of the rope.[40]

In actual fact, it is not clear how often this 'frisking'
took place or whether it is merely part of underworld
folklore. If it did occur on occasions, it was, as Mr
Shersby rightly points out, because the criminals knew
that they would all be held to be principals in the
felony of murder, even if they did not actually pull the
trigger (as in the Craig and Bentley case) and would
probably hang. However, Mr Shersby omits to mention
that it was his colleagues in Parliament that removed
this ultimate deterrent, against strong public opinion. It
may be argued that, had the death penalty remained a
possibility, the present escalation of shootings might
not have occurred. As for arming the police playing
into the hands of 'the violent minority of criminals that
carry arms' it is difficult to see the basis for this
argument. If they are already carrying arms, whether or
not the police themselves carry them, would seem to be
irrelevant. The question is whether those criminals
who at present eschew the use of firearms, would resort
to their use if they knew the police were routinely
armed. While there is certainly a possibility of this, if
the police were to adhere to the usual strict policy of
firing only when their lives or the life of another was in
danger, the fact that the pursuing or arresting
policeman carried a gun would be neither here nor
there. In fact, an unarmed criminal would, in principle,
be in no danger of being shot, even if he tried to evade
his captors. However, criminals would be aware that,
if they carried a gun, the police would have certain
prima facie grounds for believing that their intention

was to use it to endanger life. If a criminal decides to go on a job 'tooled up', it may be assumed that his intention is to use his weapon, probably to avoid arrest by firing on police officers or others if necessary. Anyone foolhardy enough actually to fire on an armed policeman knows that, unless he can be sure of completely disabling his adversary, he will almost certainly be involved in a shoot-out and risk being killed or severely injured with but a limited chance of escaping justice.

It would seem that armed police officers would be most at risk where (*a*) they are alone (or perhaps with just one colleague); (*b*) where they are taken by surprise and have no chance to defend themselves; and/or (*c*) when they are faced with a number of desperate and determined criminals. The case of Constable Patrick Dunne in 1993 illustrates this last point. When this unfortunate officer came upon some drug dealers they, without hesitation, shot him down in cold blood. There is little doubt that, had he been armed, it would have made little difference as he would have had no warning or time to draw his weapon before being killed himself. The offenders had no reason to suppose that he was armed and fired merely to evade arrest – or perhaps from pure blood lust as the mere threat of the gun would probably have dissuaded the unarmed officer from attempting to pursue the arrest of the suspects. Indeed, research carried out in the United States by the FBI shows that, while there is a typical profile of a 'cop killer', there is also a less typical but nevertheless identifiable type of officer who is likely to be the victim. It is often the good-natured and trusting police officer who gets gunned down.[41]

It may therefore be assumed that the routine arming of the police will only encourage criminals to arm themselves where they anticipate, and are willing to get involved in, a shoot-out – probably a fairly rare occurrence in the United Kingdom. But it is indeed in this scenario that the second danger might arise: that to innocent bystanders. Michael Shersby in the article referred to above says that 'if criminals knew the police were armed they would be far more likely to use their guns without restraint knowing they had nothing to lose. There would also be a high risk to the public being injured or killed in the crossfire.'[42] Here he is on much safer ground. Certainly any shooting match between cops and robbers, good guys and bad guys, is bound to give rise to the possibility of someone else getting hurt. Accurate statistics of the number of persons killed or injured in this way are not readily available as there is seldom, if ever, a discrete category of 'bystanders injured/killed in gun battles with law enforcement officers', or something similar. The victims would normally be classified as simply the victims of crime where the criminal was responsible and, where the police were concerned, it would be difficult to differentiate between innocent spectators or passers-by and possible suspects, at least for statistical purposes. Was that man who was standing outside the bank when it was robbed completely innocent or was he a non-participating accomplice to the crime?

The judicial dangers facing an armed police officer were mentioned in the last chapter with regard to the Clegg case and the more recent affair involving Constable Patrick Hodgson highlights this problem. In February, 1995, an armed response vehicle attempted to stop a stolen car outside an off-licence in Barnes, south-west London. At the wheel was David Ewin, aged 38, a man with a long string of previous convictions for robbery, possessing firearms, burglary and violence. Described as 'highly dangerous', Ewin was known to carry guns and was cleared of a charge of murder in 1985. Ewin refused to stop when challenged by the crew of the police car and attempted to drive off.

Constable Hodgson, a member of the crew, tried to stop him and, at one point, was clinging to the stolen car. In the course of the incident, Constable Hodgson apparently fired twice at Ewin, who subsequently died in hospital from his wounds. In October 1995 Constable Hodgson was charged with the murder of Ewin – the first time a serving police officer has been so charged in connection with an incident which arose in the course of his duty.

At the time of writing, the case is still before the courts and the details and final disposal are unknown, but it is obviously a case which will be followed closely by all who support or are opposed to the arming of the police in Britain.

And then there are the mistakes. Mistakes and accidents will, and do, happen, even given the limited number of occasions on which police officers are armed in this country. The Stephen Waldorf affair has already been mentioned, but there have been other regrettable incidents, such as that involving Mrs Cherry Groce in London in September 1985 which provoked a series of violent demonstrations.

Although nothing can prevent the occasional mistake or excess of zeal, the possibility of accidents can be reduced only by a high level of training, both in the handling of weapons and in their actual use. Casual and careless handling of a lethal weapon increases the danger of accidents by the inadvertent pulling of the trigger, while lack of training in the use of firearms may lead to the wrong persons becoming victims, as in the Waldorf case. At the moment it is fair to say that all authorized police firearms users are highly trained and have been psychologically screened. This entails a heavy burden of regular and intensive training; if firearms are issued to all policemen and women then this level of training – or something close to it – will need to be extended to every member of the force. The time and money involved would be enormous and while officers are undergoing training they are not out performing normal police duties. In other words, to maintain the already low levels of operational, or street, policing, there would need to be a significant increase in police strengths to cover for those officers unavailable through training commitments.

Another factor which has become increasingly pertinent is the use of imitation or replica firearms. Considerable public concern is expressed in cases such as the killing of Ian Bennett at his home in Rastrick, West Yorkshire who was found to have been armed with nothing more lethal than a replica rifle. As Bill Hughes the West Yorkshire assistant chief constable responsible for operations at the time said, 'It is impossible for police to tell it is a replica without close examination. Those who carry replica weapons must realize it is a very dangerous practice.'[43]

As mentioned in the last chapter, a similar incident occurred in Telford, Shropshire in late 1991 when police officers shot dead Ian Gordon who was threatening to shoot them. When he raised his weapon and pointed it at two of the officers saying, 'You're dead!' they both fired and it was Gordon who fell dead. It later appeared that his weapon was, in fact, a non-working air pistol, but this, of course, was not apparent to the officers. The jury at the subsequent inquest returned a verdict of lawful killing.

The unfortunate incident involving Robert Dixon further illustrates this point. It was in the early hours of the morning, just after Christmas 1994, that police armed response vehicles were called to a bungalow in Golcar, near Huddersfield where it had been reported that shots had been fired. Police officers, including eight marksmen, surrounded the house. A man was seen at a window and the police used a loud hailer to tell him that he would not be hurt if he came out immediately. This man came to the door, shouted abuse and then went back inside. He returned shortly afterwards and drew a silver revolver from his waistband, shouting, 'I'm going to blow you away!' and fired two shots towards the car behind which the negotiator was sheltering. Two police marksmen immediately opened fire with their Heckler & Koch carbines, hitting the man, Robert Dixon, five times. He died almost immediately. It was only after Dixon had been killed that the police were able to approach and discover that the revolver he had used could fire only blanks. Dixon was, in fact, a Wild West fan and amateur gunslinger. He prided himself on his quick-draw ability and had won many competitions and performed for charitable causes. He was not a violent man and had no record of this sort of behaviour and it seemed possible that he had suffered some sort of mental breakdown. However, so far as the police were concerned, they were faced with what appeared to be an armed man who fired directly at them. Few would deny that they had little option but to fire back in order to prevent the bloodshed of innocent people, especially as it was known that Dixon's disabled wife was in the house with him.

The research carried out by the Oxford University Centre for Criminological Research mentioned earlier disclosed that only one-third of convicted armed robbers admitted to have been carrying a real, loaded firearm; the others were using replicas or imitations. It is not only in this country that the problem occurs. In Germany there have been numerous incidents involving imitation and replica firearms. In January 1990 a young criminal who was holding the driver and passengers in a bus hostage was overwhelmed by police, without their having to resort to shooting him. His weapon was a replica revolver, capable of firing tear gas rounds. In January 1991, following a family dispute, a youth threatened to shoot anyone who entered his room. When he emerged pointing his pistol at the surrounding police he was shot dead. His weapon: another replica. In December 1991 an armed man was shot and wounded by police after a domestic dispute; it was later revealed that his weapon too was a gas-firing replica. In November 1990 the husband of a murder victim was stopped by the police. He produced a gun and shot and seriously wounded a policewoman before fleeing. He was pursued and several warning shots were fired before he turned and aimed his gun at his pursuers who promptly shot and killed him. His gun, another replica constructed to fire tear-gas ammunition, had actually been converted to fire live rounds. Cunningly made imitation firearms have also been used in Germany (as elsewhere). Two prison escapers took a man and a woman hostage to aid their escape, threatening them with a Beretta F92 pistol, the type of weapon used by the US armed forces. During the escape the prisoners were both wounded by the police (the hostages luckily escaped with minor injuries) who then discovered that the realistic weapon had been made in the prison from remnants of soap and bread, blackened with shoe polish. So accurate was the imitation, the prisoners had even fashioned the hammer in the full cock position! A tightening of the firearms law in Germany has led to a marked decrease in the number of cases in which a firearm was discharged (nearly 13,000 in 1971; only 4,500 in 1991); but, coincidentally, the number of occasions on which firearms were used to threaten (whether real or imitation, there is no way of telling) increased by some 30 per cent. The inference is that the stricter controls on real firearms have led to a marked increase in imitations, replicas or unusable firearms.

This is a problem for which there can really be only one answer; anyone using an imitation or replica firearm in a threatening manner must expect to be treated exactly the same as anyone with a real firearm. It would be unfair – indeed, impossible – to expect the police to examine every firearm brandished by a suspect to ensure that it was indeed a lethal weapon before they opened fire. In fact, as illustrated in some of the German cases outlined above, some replicas may be adapted fairly simply to fire a lethal missile of some sort.

Another objection to the arming of British police officers on a routine basis is that it will erode public support and confidence. This is a difficult contention to confirm or to deny and may only be based on public opinion polls or an instinctive feeling. The sight of an obviously gun-toting officer may well be distressing to some, particularly those of a nervous nature; but one wonders what would be the effect of a concealed weapon, worn under the jacket in the manner of some European countries. Probably none at all, other than on those who are opposed to the police's being armed on principle.

On the other hand, those sections of the community frequently at odds with the police – the young, the unemployed, blacks, and other generally economically-disadvantaged persons on the fringes of society – are indeed likely to have their relations with the police placed under even greater strain. Research in the US shows that the black death rate from police shootings is about nine times that for white suspects, even though the black population is around ten per cent of the total. And, as Robert Reiner points out,[44] the British evidence all points in the same direction. Being young, male, black, unemployed and economically disadvantaged are all associated with a higher probability of being stopped, searched, arrested and charged and it may be assumed that they would also be the likely targets of police shootings.

So, while the middle classes may regret their policemen bearing arms, especially if the weapons are visible, they are not likely to be involved in a shooting (except where they are merely innocent bystanders), whereas the lower working class and marginal groups will be in greater danger, especially if they perceive a need to carry arms themselves.

Another unwelcome spin-off of arming the police are the traumas suffered by the police themselves when they are involved in a shooting. As former police psychologist Dr Ian McKenzie found during a period of attachment to the Fort Worth (Texas) police department, 'To be involved in a shooting, at either end of the gun, is, in the jargon of psychology, a "traumatic incident" of the first order.'[45] It causes the police officer to react in unusual ways; some are driven to suicide or to threaten to kill themselves, their spouses or members of their family. Others reach for their gun on the slightest unusual noise, such as a car backfiring.

The final objection to the arming of the British police is that this country would rapidly become like the United States, with shootings and shoot-outs being commonplace. But is this a reasonable supposition? It has been said that 'it is the truest of truisms that the United States is a nation obsessed with guns – and nowhere more so than among the cops themselves.'[46] This is not the case in the United Kingdom (or in almost any other developed country) and, if we are to examine the possible repercussions of an armed police service we should be looking much closer to home; to the police forces in Europe and the Anglo-Saxon countries of Australia and New Zealand and even Canada which, although sharing many of its neighbour's traits, is quite different in other ways.

In the next chapter we shall be looking at these countries in more depth and comparing them with the United Kingdom and the United States.

6 Abroad is unutterably bloody!

There are many who would share the view of Nancy Mitford's Lord Alconleigh concerning all things foreign, as expressed in the heading of this chapter, and this distrust of foreign ways extends to the employment of armed police officers. So deeply entrenched is this attitude that no less a personage than the Parliamentary Adviser to the Police Federation, Michael Shersby, has expressed the view that:

> In many countries where the police are armed, the criminal use of firearms is much greater. This means that many more officers are killed or injured by gunfire than in Britain and there are more incidents in which the police kill or injure criminals and sometimes innocent bystanders.[47]

Unfortunately Mr Shersby does not provide any statistics to support this statement and, unless he is referring to the United States and perhaps some South American or Third World countries, it is questionable whether these assertions are borne out by facts or are mere impressions. The aim of this chapter is to examine the situation in a number of other countries to try to determine just what the facts are.

Let us begin by considering the United States. It seems that whenever the question of arming the police in this country is raised, the knee-jerk reaction is to point to the American experience. And it is certainly a salutary example. As mentioned in the last chapter, 'the United States is a nation obsessed with guns'.

In 1992 a total of 1,932,274 violent crimes were

committed there, equal to 757.5 for every 100,000 of the population. Of these, 23,760 (9.3 per 100,000) were murders or manslaughters, 672,478 (263.6 per 100,000) were robberies and 1,126,974 (441.8 per 100,000) serious assaults.

As one might expect, firearms were used in two-thirds of the murders, mostly handguns. One major difference between the USA and the UK (which reflects the more ready availability of handguns in the USA) is the fact that shotguns represented a mere ten per cent of the weapons in the United States, whereas this type of weapon is much more common here. In the United States firearms of one sort or another were used in 40 per cent of the cases of robbery.

These figures compare with the following approximate total figures for comparable crimes in the UK as follows:

murder/manslaughter	678
robbery	45,000
grievous bodily harm/wounding	10,000

Taken as a percentage of the population, the comparison is shown in Table 2:

TABLE 2
CRIME COMPARISONS USA* AND UK†

Per 100.000 inhabitants [firearms used]		
	UK	USA
Homicide	1.36 [9%]	9.30 [68.2%]
Robberies	90.16	263.60 [40%]
Serious assaults	20.00	441.80 [25%]
Number of officers killed in the line of duty	0.0036 [45%]	0.0255 [94%]

Notes
* 1992
† average 1989–93

So far as the police are concerned, in the USA around 65 law-enforcement officers are killed each year (average of 1991/92), which represents roughly one officer killed for every 8,540 law-enforcement officers. This is roughly eight times as many as in England and Wales (1:69,500). The vast majority (94 per cent) of the US officers were killed by the use of a firearm (again mostly handguns). What the United States experience does perhaps highlight is the particular vulnerability of police officers working alone. In 70 per cent of reported cases the victim was alone at the time of the killing.[48]

Since the *Uniform Crime Reports* published by the US Department of Justice do not quote the number of persons shot by the police, let us look at figures supplied by the New York Police Department. Although the crime and other figures for New York are on the high side, they may nevertheless be extrapolated to give an idea of the nation as a whole. Each year in New York there are some 520 occasions on which shots are fired at criminals or suspects (about 18.6 occasions per 1,000 police officers), resulting in an average of 28 individuals being shot dead (roughly one for every 1,000 officers) and a further 69 or so being injured.

Given that the population and police establishment in New York are both closely similar to those of London, the wide difference may be readily appreciated. But, of course, New York is not the United States any more than London is England. In fact, the number of murders (and other violent crimes) is roughly double the national average and so one might expect the number of occasions on which firearms are used by the New York Police Department to be double that for the rest of that country. If this is indeed the case, then the average number of occasions on which firearms are used by police officers throughout the United States would be around ten per 1,000 officers. Taking this hypothesis further, this would suggest that there are 50 killings of suspects each year for every 100,000 law enforcement officers in the United States.

What about other countries? Some figures have been obtained from those responsible for policing France, Germany, the Netherlands, Belgium, Norway, Sweden, Spain, New Zealand, Australia and Canada. In some cases, especially where there are a number of police forces, possibly coming under different government departments, it has been necessary to estimate the figures by extrapolation from those available and, where this is the case, the country is flagged by an asterisk[*].

The first figure to be considered is the ratio of police to members of the public. As will be seen from Table 3, the ratio for England and Wales is very close to the average.

TABLE 3
POLICE AND POPULATION

Country	Population (millions)	Police strength	Ratio police/ inhabitants
England and Wales[1]	50.50	125,000	1:404
France*	55.90	213,000	1:262
Germany*	78.30	250,000	1:313
Netherlands*	14.82	30,000	1:494
Belgium*	9.87	31,650	1:312
Norway[1]	4.23	6,500	1:650
Sweden	8.53	17,750	1:480
Spain*	39.00	130,000	1:300
New Zealand[1]	3.36	6,900	1:487
Australia*	12.25	30,000	1:408
Canada	26.22	56,880	1:461

Notes
1. These forces are normally unarmed.
* See note in text

112

The wide variations in the ratio of police to the public (1:26 to 1:65) may be partly explained by differences in the definition of a police officer. In some continental towns, for example, the municipal police are almost entirely concerned with traffic control, parking and local bye-laws and are more like our traffic wardens than regular police officers. In the case of France, which appears to have the lowest police:population ratio, the number of police officers quoted includes members of the National Gendarmerie which carries out duties in addition to what one might regard as 'normal' policing. It provides the military police function, both in France and in overseas military stations and also includes the Garde Républicaine which is closer to the Household Cavalry than the British Bobby. It is not clear why the ratio in Norway is so high, although, given its sparse and scattered population, the authorities may have seen no need for a substantial reserve for public order incidents. The average over this group is 1:42.

It is often said that (a) we are living in violent times, in (b) a violent country. The extent to which the first contention is true has been addressed in the first chapter, and the reader will make his or her own mind up as to whether our times are indeed more violent than earlier ones.

The second suggestion, that British society is a violent one, means that some comparisons have to be made with other countries. Just how to define levels of violence is a difficult matter; the number of murders/manslaughters is one figure we may use; the number of robberies is another. The use of figures for cases of assault is much more complex. The concept of violence ranges from a simple slap to the inflicting of life-threatening injuries, such as wounding and grievous bodily harm and the classification of such crimes depends on the law and custom of the country with

113

which one is attempting to make a comparison. Several countries use terms such as 'aggravated assault', others divide the statistics into those committed against specified categories of persons or property. My own investigations have led me to the conclusion that the use of such figures as are available would not provide a useful comparison and could, indeed, be seriously misleading. I have therefore taken the figures relating to murders and robberies to illustrate the levels of 'violent crime' in a number of countries; see Table 4

TABLE 4
COMPARISON OF VIOLENT CRIME FIGURES
(PER 100,000 INHABITANTS)

Country	Homicides	Robberies
England and Wales	1.23	89.10
France	4.35	86.30
Germany	3.11	40.29
Netherlands	N/A	N/A
Belgium	1.47	N/A
Norway	0.28	4.08
Sweden	2.00	73.00
Spain	N/A	N/A
New Zealand	2.60	41.66
Australia	1.70	75.00
Canada	N/A	N/A
USA	93.12	263.60

Fortunately, the actual number of homicides is generally low and the statistics shown in the table must therefore be viewed with caution, especially where the smaller countries are concerned since they may be radically influenced by a single incident.

What will be seen is that France appears to have a high rate of homicide; in fact, ignoring the incredible figures for the United States, provided by way of comparison, it shows the highest rate of all the countries surveyed. However, it must be pointed out that the only available figures for that country were for 1987 and the use of one year only may be misleading, especially where the total number of cases is, in any case, fairly low. In other words, this could just have been a bad year for France.

In fact, there are indications that throughout Europe the incidence of violent crime has generally been dropping over recent years. For example, in West Germany (before unification) the criminal use of firearms peaked in 1977 with 21,000 cases and, with minor peaks (never exceeding 17,000), it has been declining ever since and, by 1990, was under 11,000. The police in Germany are, of course, routinely armed.

The figures for robberies are also to be used with caution since the definition of this offence varies widely from one country to another. With the otherwise inexplicable variations in the case of Norway (which coincidentally is the smallest unit included), the average for most of the European countries and the Antipodes is very similar. The lowest is New Zealand which has been enjoying several years of economic stability but there are clear indications that, as this country falls into recession, the crime figures there are rising markedly and by the time these words are read they may have caught up with the remainder of the countries surveyed.

What this table clearly shows is the fact that crime in the countries surveyed is remarkably similar and, in every case, very much lower than that in the United States, which confirms the original contention that that country is not a good one with which to make comparisons.

How about the police? Of the countries surveyed, only three are not routinely armed: England and Wales,

Norway and New Zealand. Does this have an effect on (a) the general rates of violent crime and (b) the vulnerability of the officers on the streets?

The answer to (a) must be that it appears to make little difference. One might compare Norway (unarmed) with neighbouring Sweden (armed) to conclude that the lack of police firearms is definitely beneficial, but then one could compare New Zealand (unarmed) with very similar Australia (armed) to show that the latter has a lower homicide rate. Given the already mentioned unreliability of the robbery figures, the prima-facie inference drawn from these is that the unarmed British police face violent crime levels similar to their French and Australian counterparts, both of whom are armed.

If crime rates are fairly uniform, are the police themselves more at risk without the benefit of firearms? It is fair to assume that the more police officers there are, the more they are at risk and so the figures given below relate to *police strengths* and not to population (although there is a fairly close corollary as we saw in Table 3). Averaged out over five years, the comparison is as shown in Table 5.

Given the low number of actual police victims (only in the US do these reach double figures; in no other country does it exceed three), a single casualty may make a big difference to the ratio. In the same way, the relevance of firearms use is much influenced by the low numbers. Over five years only one police officer was killed (by a firearm) in Sweden and the same in Norway, while two were killed in Australia, again involving the use of firearms, giving 100 per cent figures in every case. It is feasible to speculate that, over another period of five years, an officer in one of these countries could be killed by the use of a knife or other means and none by shooting, which would completely reverse the proportions.

TABLE 5
POLICE OFFICERS KILLED/INJURED BY CRIMINAL
ACTIVITY (ANNUAL AVERAGE PER 100,000 OFFICERS)

Country	Deaths by firearms		Injured by firearms
England and Wales	1.44	(44.5%)	N/A
France*	2.58	(75%)	19.80
Germany*	3.125	(100%)	19.44
Netherlands*	1.6	(100%)	N/A
Belgium*	7.5	(100%)	28.75
Norway	3.33	(100%)	3.33
Sweden	1.10	(100%)	3.33
Spain*	1.70	(N/A)	N/A
New Zealand	5.70[1]	(50%)	2.85
Australia*	1.33	(100%)	8.66
Canada	N/A	(N/A)	N/A
USA	11.71	(94%)	N/A

Notes
1. Although this appears rather high, there were in fact only two
officers killed during the five years.
* See note to Table 3 in text.

It is not possible to give any reason for the
comparatively high number of officers killed in
Belgium. The actual casualties sustained by the Belgian
Gendarmerie (representing roughly half the total police
strength) was six over five years which, given the size
of the country, is a high figure, although it may be
balanced to a certain extent by a low casualty rate in
the municipal police forces (for which no figures are
available). Does the fact that the arms controls in
Belgium are among the most liberal in Europe have any
bearing on this apparent anomaly?

The important point to be extracted from these
figures is that, with the exception of the anomalies
mentioned above, and always leaving the United States

to one side, the average figures are remarkably similar, ranging from a low of 1.1 in Sweden to a high of 3.33 in Norway. The unarmed police forces (England and Wales, Norway and New Zealand) figure third, eighth and ninth in an ascending list of 12 countries. It therefore cannot be said that England and Wales, with the third lowest police casualty rate, suffers unduly from the lack of personal weapons. Of course, any casualty is to be deplored and it may be that the routine issuing of firearms to these officers would reduce these figures still further, but there would not appear to be any grounds for panic measures and any possible advantages must be viewed against the perceived disadvantages.

Finally, with regard to the question of an officer's weapons being used against him or his colleagues, with the exception of the United States, this appears to be an insignificant problem. Only in France (one killed and two injured over five years) were any cases reported. In New York City one officer was killed and 11 were injured by police weapons over the same period. The inference would seem to be that, with proper care, it is unlikely that the arming of a police officer will prove directly responsible for his death or injury.

Which brings us to the use of firearms by the police and the possible danger to the public. Table 6 shows the average number of occasions that officers of the force concerned shot at and killed a suspect, and shot and wounded a suspect.

At first sight the British practice of employing unarmed police officers, other than in certain, limited circumstances, appears to pay off and the number of persons killed or injured by the police in England and Wales is extremely small, especially when compared with other countries. On the other hand, the number of incidents involving the normally unarmed New Zealand police are among the highest! However, we

come back to the disparity of force sizes, the New
Zealand force being one of the smaller with only some
7,000 officers for the whole country. In plain figures,
there were only three deaths and two injuries from
police action in New Zealand during the whole of the
five years reviewed (which is still quite high for a
population of 3,360,000).

TABLE 6
SUSPECTS KILLED/INJURED BY POLICE USE OF FIREARMS
OVER FIVE YEARS (CASES PER 100,000 OFFICERS)

Country	Suspects killed	Suspects injured
England and Wales	1.60	2.40
France	19.00	67.37
Germany	22.40	740.00
Netherlands	42.00	N/A
Belgium	26.60	140.00
Norway	N/A	N/A
Sweden	28.00	197.00
Spain	N/A	N/A
New Zealand	48.25	285.00
Australia	38.00	111.50
Canada	100.00	225.00
USA (estimated)	285.00	68.00

In fact, when one analyses the figures, those for the
European countries (France, Germany, Belgium and
Sweden) are remarkably similar (between 19 and 28
cases of death by shooting). Only the Netherlands has
produced unusually high figures and it is not clear why
this should be so. It has to be admitted that, because of
a wide-ranging reorganization of the police service
recently carried out in the Netherlands, a great many
valuable records and statistics have been lost or

destroyed and the figures quoted are based on estimates made by the Free University of Amsterdam Centre for Police Studies. There is no reason to suppose, however, that these estimates are in any way unreliable.

The incidence of police shootings in both Australia and New Zealand is comparatively high (38 and 48.25 per 100,000 police officers), while Canada is even higher with 100 fatal shootings. Again, no attempt has been made to rationalize these discrepancies; indeed, a whole study could easily be made of the reasons for shooting at suspects and the results of these. It may be that these comparatively young countries are still suffering from the pioneer spirit and the lawlessness which often accompanies newly settled lands.

What is clear, once more, is that the United States (another pioneer nation?) by far outstrips all the other countries surveyed, with more than five times the number of cases its Canadian neighbour has experienced, more than ten times the Antipodean countries, and something like 20 times the number of killings in western Europe.

There appear to be few records which demonstrate whether those suspects who were shot were indeed criminals or were presenting a threat. The rules in most, if not all, countries are extremely rigid regarding the circumstances in which a police officer may open fire, usually involving a tangible threat of death or serious injury to the officer or another person (see the Appendix). It would be foolish to suggest that none of the reported cases involved an error of identification or of judgement, but the low numbers involved, even in countries which have an armed police service, tend to suggest that the likelihood of an unjustifiable shooting is negligible (with the possible exception of the United States, where the high level of violent crime could result in individual police officers taking an assertive rather than a reactive stance, perceiving a threat where no real danger exists).

All one can say is that, if all the individuals killed or wounded by the police represented a positive threat to the life of another, it must be assumed that the shooting of these 'victims' resulted in the saving of the lives of either the police officers concerned, or of third parties. Or at least averted possible serious injury. So, far from presenting a threat to innocent bystanders, the presence of an armed police officer is probably much more likely to save a life.

7 Conclusions

Kipling described the English in a rather jaundiced manner, writing:

> For undemocratic reasons and for motives not of state, They arrive at their conclusions – largely inarticulate.

The aim of this book is to render more articulate the views held by those who support the routine arming of the British police and those who are vehemently opposed to such a move. Whatever decision is ultimately taken, it is to be hoped that it will be arrived at with the full possession of the facts. When the decision makers – the politicians, senior police officers and judiciary – finally make their decision, one hopes that it will not be taken for undemocratic reasons and that the best interests of the state will be borne in mind, rather than short-term, political expediency.

In the preceding chapters we have examined, as far as we are able, the facts on which such a decision should be taken and an attempt has been made to dismiss pure speculation and prejudice. So what conclusions can we reasonably draw? Is British society as we enter the third millennium more violent than it has ever been? A number of factors must be borne in mind when making comparisons. First, the population of this country has grown enormously over the past two centuries, with a threefold increase in the hundred years between the middle of the nineteenth century and the middle of this century, and one must expect at least the basic crime figures to reflect this growth.

Secondly, the violent mass disorders which characterized the nineteenth century have largely disappeared and the violence which occurs in more recent times has taken on a different guise. Thirdly, the statistics used to support any particular hypothesis have to be treated with caution. No official crime statistics were kept before the nineteenth century and, when records were maintained, these were not always accurate or complete. The 'dark figure' – those offences which, for one reason or another did not come to the attention of the authorities – is always an unknown but significant factor. The fact that more crimes were reported in one year as compared with another does not necessarily mean that more crimes were committed in the first. Other factors, such as the insistence by insurance companies that losses through crime be reported to the police, have a considerable effect on the ultimate crime figures. Sentencing policies also had an effect, with juries in the last century being understandably loath to convict some less-serious felons, knowing that the penalty would automatically mean death.

Accepting all these provisos, we come to the indisputable fact that, in the course of the past century, there has been a threefold increase in the proportional number of murders. The reason for this is not immediately clear and would call for further study to determine whether, for example, there are more or fewer 'domestic' murders now than in the last century and how many murders are committed in the furtherance of other crimes. There has also been a clear explosion in the number of robberies

Taking account of all the reservations, provisos, stipulations and conditions with which crime statistics must be viewed, there would seem to have been an increase in violent crime in this country, especially in the last few decades, but this increase might not be so great as the available figures suggest. To what extent this apparent increase in violent and, in particular, deadly crimes is linked to the law regarding murder and the degree of firearms control, is something which could form the subject of another book. But it is perhaps worthy of a brief overview here.

Most observers have the impression, justified or not, that many of those who have taken the life of another 'get away' with being charged with manslaughter rather than murder. The awful vision of the judge in the black cap pronouncing the death sentence is no longer to be seen in our criminal courts and any tendency to reduce charges of murder to something less on the grounds that the punishment for the former is too dreadful to contemplate no longer has any validity.

Curiously enough, murder is a crime against the common law and there is no statutory definition of the offence. It is often described as 'unlawful homicide with malice aforethought' (per Stephen J. in *Doherty* [1887] 16 Cox CC 306) although the full description is usually accepted to be that used by Coke as long ago as 1640:

> When any man of sound memory and of the age of discretion unlawfully killeth ... any reasonable creature in being ... with malice aforethought, either expressed ... or implied by law so as the party wounded or hurt etc die of the wound or hurt etc within a year and a day after the same.

Over the years there has been little change in the interpretation of much of this definition but the expression 'malice aforethought' has been the subject of numerous judicial decisions and it is perhaps these which some would see as diminishing the crime and resulting in more and more cases being dealt with as manslaughter. The term is simply a 'comprehensive name for a number of different mental attitudes'[49] and the courts had previously held that it involved an intention to cause harm to (not necessarily to kill) another.

The Criminal Justice Act of 1967 removed this assumption that a reasonable person foresees the natural consequences of his acts and laid down that it is the actual *intention* at the time the offence is committed which is paramount. Thus, if A shoots at B with the intention of frightening him but accidentally kills him, he will not now be guilty of murder, even though the firing of a gun pointed in someone's direction might reasonably be expected to injure him or cause his death.

A further matter which might be seen to be watering down the law regarding murder is the plea of diminished responsibility which was introduced by the Homicide Act of 1957 and entitles the accused to be found guilty of manslaughter rather than murder if he is suffering from an abnormality of mind which impaired his mental responsibility for his acts.

Before the passing of this Act, only the M'Naghten Rules applied which allow for a verdict of 'guilty but insane' and permitted incarceration in a mental institution such as Broadmoor rather than hanging or life imprisonment. The new Act opened a much wider door and most offenders would naturally prefer to be convicted of manslaughter rather than be deemed insane and locked away for an indefinite time.

There is therefore no doubt that many offences which at one time would have been dealt with as murder are now treated as manslaughter. Whether or not this has had an effect on the minds of violent criminals is, of course, difficult to say. Nevertheless, the penalty for killing another human being has gradually diminished from almost certain hanging, to life imprisonment, to a long prison sentence and, finally, to what may now be seen as a comparatively minor term of imprisonment (and possibly not even that).

Since this book is largely concerned with firearms, it may also be useful to consider briefly the firearms laws and the control of these weapons in this country. The Firearms Act controls the sale and acquisition of all types of firearms and the possession and carrying of these. It prohibits certain firearms such as machine guns, rocket launchers and guns for the discharge of noxious gases or liquids and makes all other firearms (with the exception of shotguns and airguns) subject to stringent licensing requirements.

As a result, it may be said that it is extremely difficult to obtain a firearm such as a rifle or revolver *legally* in this country. Shotguns are subject to special requirements because of their sporting connotations and are much easier to acquire. There is, however, a lively trade in both unlicensed and illegal handguns as well as what might almost be described as a roaring trade in illicit shotguns, many of which are cut down to make them easier to handle. Many of these weapons are stolen in the course of burglaries while others are illegally imported from other countries where the regulations are much more lax, such as Belgium or the United States.

There will always be a place for the legal possession of firearms, whether for sporting purposes, the destruction of vermin or for use in gun clubs for target practice. It is therefore unthinkable that there should be a complete ban on all types of firearm, and such a ban would undoubtedly be circumvented by criminals. All the authorities can hope to do is make it as difficult as possible for undesirable persons to get hold of lethal weapons. Fortunately, we do not have the sort of gun lobby which exists in the United States where certain factions insist that the Constitution's reference to the right to bear arms means that there should be no restriction on the possession of firearms – with the kind of result with which we are all too familiar.

So far as the police are concerned, the aim of arming them is twofold: to protect the officer himself or herself and to protect other citizens. If we are ineluctably drawn to the view that our modern society is more violent than previously, how does this affect the police? Are lethal weapons more readily available than hitherto? Are the police more at risk than ever before?

Since there is no likelihood of police firearms being used other than where life was in danger, the relevant figure is the number of police officers killed in the line of duty. Are more policemen being killed these days and, if so, would the number be reduced if they were armed?

As we have seen in previous chapters, in general, despite the fact that there were considerably fewer police officers at that time, more policemen were killed in the nineteenth century than in most of the present one. Only in the past decade or two have the numbers of police fatalities equalled those in the decade 1871-80. So, given the perceived increase in violent crime, the number of serious (i.e., fatal) assaults on police officers does not seem to have followed this pattern. There has undoubtedly been a considerable increase in violent but non-fatal assaults on the police, at least over the last few decades but, regrettable while this may be, it is not a justification for arming them. In fact, where an armed police officer is being assaulted, the temptation for him or her to use the weapon in self-defence even when the assault is non-life threatening, could lead to an escalation in the number of victims of (unlawful) police shootings.

It may fairly be stated therefore that the number of violent crimes has increased in recent years and is still increasing. The number of police officers killed in the line of duty has also increased in the last decade but, viewed historically, the number of these is not so great as to justify any panic measures.

If, despite these considerations, the prospect of arming the police in the country as a matter of routine is pursued, what are likely to be the consequences? Will there be daily shoot-outs between the police and criminals in the streets of our cities? Will innocent bystanders be gunned down by the police by accident or mistake? Will this country become a replica of the United States?

As we have seen, the figures for crime in the United States and the police use of firearms are both alarming; what evidence is there to show that once the police in Britain are armed we would be inexorably drawn into an American style of crime and policing? In fact, there is no evidence to suggest that this is necessarily a foregone conclusion. The United States must, for reasons of history and national character, be seen as a unique case.

The police in most countries are armed and no country which has close similarities with our own has ever followed the American example. In fact, the experience in most of these countries remains similar to our own. There is no escalation of violent crime, shoot-outs are rare, as are accidental or mistaken shootings, and the number of police deaths seems little affected. What is not clear is how many non-police lives were saved by the presence of armed police officers.

To sum up, therefore, it would seem that the arming or otherwise of the police has little effect on violent crime. At present England and Wales have one of the lowest homicide records, very similar to Belgium (armed police). In New Zealand where the police are not usually armed, the number of homicides is higher than in nearby Australia where the police are armed.

The number of police officers fatally injured is

fortunately very low in all the countries surveyed and it is therefore difficult to draw any clear conclusions from the available figures, since one additional death may result in a 100 per cent increase in the total. There is certainly no hard evidence that arming the police has either a beneficial or a detrimental effect on the incidence of police deaths by criminal activity.

As might be expected, the number of 'suspects' killed and injured by the British police is very low, given the comparatively few occasions on which weapons have been available to them. What is perhaps surprising is the relatively high number of suspects killed and injured by the New Zealand police, given that they are not normally armed and are subject to strict 'rules of engagement' when they are (see the Appendix). Similarly, the number of injuries inflicted on uninvolved bystanders appears to be negligible, although the statistics are far from clear on this point.

If the decision is taken not to arm the police in England and Wales then perhaps one should be looking at better means of non-lethal protection and of subduing violent assailants. As we have seen, apart from the issuing of cutlasses in the early days of organized policing and the comparatively few occasions on which the police have had recourse to firearms, reliance has been placed almost exclusively on the truncheon. This 16-inch piece of wood (usually rosewood, occasionally lignum vitae) stems from the tipstaff which served as a symbol of office for certain parish constables and court officers. This developed into the magnificent hand-painted truncheons issued from around the seventeenth century and reaching their zenith in the late Georgian period and in the reign of William IV, examples of which may be seen in police museums and collections such as that at the Police Staff College at Bramshill. As time went on and the police became organized and began to wear a clearly recognizable uniform, the truncheon became more and more a weapon of defence (and sometimes offence). It has served the police well but is it adequate against the more sophisticated weapons used by the criminal elements of today? Most police officers will answer that question with a resounding 'no'. Whether or not individual police officers wish to bear arms, there is virtual unanimity in the view that some better form of protection is necessary. The uniform, which itself served as real protection in the recent past, has now become more a target.

The commercial and industrial interests have not been slow in answering this plea for better weapons, especially in the United States, and several alternative, non-lethal weapons have been proposed and are available. These vary from variations on the theme of the truncheon to non-lethal, non-contact weapons such as gas or pepper sprays.

The latest versions of the truncheon include side-handled, steel-cored, epoxy resin batons and straight, telescopic batons. The former, being longer than the traditional, wooden version, cannot reasonably be concealed in the special trouser pocket and thus must be carried in an overt and, some would say, aggressive manner. The telescopic version is more portable but must be extended before use, usually by a powerful flicking movement (known as 'racking'). This very action has been observed to discourage threatened assaults, since the extended baton (which may be up to 21 inches long) is obviously a formidable weapon exerting approximately twice the power that could be applied by the traditional truncheon. The design of the side-handled baton in particular facilitates its use to deflect attacks by knife or blunt instrument, but the main problem with these protective devices is the fact that considerable training is required if they are to be used effectively.

Extensive trials have been, and continue to be,

carried out in a number of police forces in Great Britain but so far no clear preference has emerged. In fact, where both types are subject to trial in parallel, half the users prefer the telescopic baton while others plump for the side-handled version. So, at the time of writing 'the jury is out' and it seems likely that each of the 43 forces will make its own decision.

But batons are not the only alternative to firearms or other lethal weapons and a wide variety of 'less than lethal force' weapons are being offered, especially in America. These include electrical prods (of the type used to herd animals), dazzle lights and stun grenades, but the most practical and probably the most acceptable weapons available to the police armoury are the varieties of non-lethal spray. These may use CS gas or capsicum pepper or some other substance. Organic, non-chemical substances, such as pepper, are usually preferred to synthetic chemical products although there have been suggestions that the capsicum pepper sprays, now used fairly widely in the United States, may be carcinogenic or otherwise dangerous, especially to those who already have respiratory or other health problems.

At the time of writing, the most favoured possibility seems to be some type of tear gas spray, and in March 1996 16 forces began to deploy CS gas canisters. Tests are also being carried out on what has been described as a 'Spiderman gun' which engulfs troublemakers in a disabling web, and an equally exotic splatter gun which shoots jelly at a force described as being equal to a right hook from a heavyweight boxer. Also being reviewed is a shotgun which fires bean bags instead of pellets. Although some of these weapons sound more like something from *Blue Peter* or *Doctor Who*, who knows what the future will hold? It could be very interesting!

Whatever weapons are eventually incorporated into

the police arsenal in this country, public reaction must be taken into account. Mention has been made of the necessity to carry the new-style batons in an overt manner which, although it might deter some malevolent persons, might also offend the susceptibilities of the law-abiding public almost as much as the visible carrying of firearms. It is true, however, that a public opinion survey showed that 70 per cent of the public were in favour of the police using the new style batons. This reaction probably stems from the widespread fear of violent crime which many honest citizens hold.

What, then, should be the police response to progressive non-compliance and aggression? The Americans have produced a 'Use of Force Continuum' which generally suggests that police response should directly reflect the level of opposition met. This may be summarized as follows:

Level of resistance	*Police response*
minor misbehaviour	presence of police officer
non-compliance	verbal direction
passive resistance	empty hands control
active resistance	display of baton/handcuffs
active aggression	strikes with baton
lethal threat	use of firearms

It is held that if the police response does not match the level of resistance it will either prove ineffective (if the response is too low) or excessive (if the response is too high). The balance is a fine one but the police have been adopting similar responses (excluding the use of firearms in our case) for many years. What is slightly worrying is the possibility that, if the police are issued with the non-lethal weapons described earlier, there may be a tendency to use these at a much earlier stage than that where one would have resorted to the use of the baton – and certainly much sooner than one at which the use of firearms would have been contemplated.

So there we are. Has the case been made for the routine arming of the police in Great Britain, or would the introduction of other, non-lethal weapons prove adequate? What is to be the image of British police officers in the next century? Are they going to emulate their American counterparts, model themselves on their EU colleagues, or keep an independent and different profile, albeit not the traditional one? And who should decide – the police themselves, the public, or the politicians?

The announcement by the Prime Minister John Major of the intention to form a British 'FBI' immediately raises questions as to whether its members, like their American counterparts, are to be routinely armed. As one unidentified member of SO19 is reported to have said, 'A British FBI would be powerless without the proper armed back-up.'[50]

A great many questions are therefore posed and it is not the intention that this book should reach any hard and fast conclusions. What is hoped is that it has cleared the air and set out the pros and cons of the debate in an unbiased and disinterested manner. It is now up to the jury to reach their verdict.

Appendix:
The New Zealand Police 'Rules of Engagement'

As has been mentioned previously, most if not all police forces have strict rules governing the use of firearms by the police. Although these will obviously vary from force to force and from country to country (and possibly in response to the perceived dangers), the following edited extract from the New Zealand Police Standing Orders provides a good and fairly typical example of the 'rules of engagement' laid down for the police.

F61 *Use of Firearms by Police*

(1) Members must always be aware of their personal responsibilities in the use of firearms. ... a member is criminally liable for excess force. An overriding requirement in law is that minimum force must be applied to effect the purpose. Police should not use a firearm unless it can be done without endangering other persons.

(2) Police members shall not use a firearm except in the following circumstances:

(a) To defend themselves or others if they fear death or grievous bodily harm to themselves or others, and they cannot reasonably protect themselves, or others, in a less violent manner.

(b) To ARREST an offender if they believe on reasonable grounds that the offender poses a threat of death or grievous bodily harm in resisting his arrest
AND
the arrest cannot reasonably be effected in a less

> violent manner
> AND
> the arrest cannot be delayed without danger to other persons.

(c) To PREVENT THE ESCAPE of an offender if it is believed on reasonable grounds that the offender poses a threat of death or grievous bodily harm to any person (whether an identifiable individual or members of the public at large)
AND
he takes flight to avoid arrest, OR he escapes after arrest
AND
such flight of escape cannot reasonably be prevented in a less violent manner.

(3) In any case, an offender is not to be shot:

(a) until he has first been called upon to surrender, unless in the circumstances it is impracticable and unsafe to do so,
AND

(b) It is clear that he cannot be disarmed or arrested without the use of firearms
AND

(c) in the circumstances, further delay in apprehending him would be dangerous or impracticable.

F62 *Fire Orders*
Every sworn member of Police who is issued with a firearm in the course of duty shall ensure that he or she is thoroughly conversant with the provisions of General Instruction F61.

F63 *Police Firearms*
In addition to the circumstances set out in General Instruction F61, the police may use firearms:
(a) To destroy animals in circumstances set out in the

Manual of Police Practice, and
(b)   for training purposes.

F64 *Warning shots*
As a general rule, warning shots should never be fired. However, there may be circumstances as outlined in GI F61 where a warning shot may be appropriate.

The following principles must always be borne in mind:
(a)   Extreme caution is taken to safeguard the lives of others, and
(b)   the offender has, where practicable, been called upon to surrender and has failed to do so, and
(c)   the shot can clearly be aimed as a warning shot, i.e. vertically in the air, in the open, or at an equally safe target elsewhere so as to safeguard the public and plainly demonstrate to the offender that he is in fact receiving a warning and not being shot at. Any misconception in this regard may precipitate the offending action that a warning shot is trying to prevent.

F65 *Shooting at Motor Vehicles*
Shots shall not be fired at moving vehicles except in very exceptional circumstances. It is extremely difficult to disable a vehicle by discharging a firearm aimed at the tyres or other parts. The small target area and the margin for error imposes a high probability of misdirection or ricochet and the risk of causing death, injury or damage cannot be over-emphasised.

F66 *Discharge of Firearms by Police to be Reported*
(1)   On each occasion that a member discharges a firearm in the course of duty, whether deliberately or accidentally, other than during training or destroying animals, he shall:

(*a*) Preserve the cartridge case and where possible the bullet or bullet fragments associated with the firearm;

(*b*) Secure the firearm and remaining rounds;

(*c*) As far as is practicable, secure the immediate area;

(*d*) Promptly notify his immediate supervisor who shall notify the District Commander.

(2) Where the member discharging a firearm is at the time one of a squad engaged on a specific operation, the member in charge shall, in addition to ensuring that the matters in clause (1)(*a*) to (*d*) hereof are completed, mark the position of the firer, empty cartridge case, bullet fragments, injured or deceased persons, or any other items or persons associated with the shooting.

(3) As soon as practicable, such firearms, bullets or fragments are to be handed to an NCO or Commissioned Officer for custody.

(4) The District Commander will forward to the Assistant Commissioner a brief summary of the facts.

(5) Should the circumstance so dictate, the firearm is to be forwarded to the Police Armoury for examination.

(6) The District Commander shall have inquiries made and forward the file, with recommendations, to the Assistant Commissioner.

Notes

1. M. Madan, *Thoughts on Executive Justice* ... (London, 1785).
2. H. McRae, *The World in 2020* (London: Harper/Collins, 1994).
3. C. Emsley, *Crime and Society in England 1750–1900* (London: Longman, 1987).
4. J. Hanway, *The Defects of the Police* (London, 1775), p. 224.
5. W.L. Melville Lee, *A History of Police in England* (London: Methuen, 1901).
6. *Chester Chronicle*, 13 March 1829.
7. P. Colquhoun, *Treatise on the Police of the Metropolis* (London, 1796), p. vii.
8. E. Chadwick, MSS *Police Memoranda, etc.* (London: University College, undated: post 1850).
9. C. Emsley, op. cit.
10. R. Ingleton, *The Gentlemen at War: Policing Britain 1939–45* (Maidstone: Cranborne Publications, 1994).
11. *Police* (Sept. 1994), p. 17.
12. Bedfordshire Records Office QSR 1827/338.
13. C. Emsley, *The English Police* (Hemel Hempstead: Harvester Wheatsheaf, 1991).
14. C. Emsley, ibid.
15. F.P. Wensley, *Detective Days* (London: Cassell, 1931).
16. J. White, *The Worst Street in North London* (London: Routledge & Kegan Paul, 1986).
17. *Justice of the Peace*, XCI (1927), p. 489.
18. R. Ingleton, op. cit.
19. R.W. Gould and M.J. Waldren, *London's Armed Police* (London: Arms & Armour Press, 1986).
20. *First Report of the Commissioners of the Metropolitan Police*, PP 1839 (169) XIX, p. 83.
21. Earl Gray, Lords *Hansard*, CXXII (15 June 1852), cols. 748–9.
22. *First Report of the Select Committee on the Police*, PP 1852–53 (603) XXXVI, pp. 166, 217.
23. *Evening Standard* (29 Aug. 1883).
24. *Daily Telegraph* (27 Sept. 1883).
25. *The Police Review* (23 Jan. 1893), p. 37.
26. *Justice of the Peace*, XCV (5 Dec. 1931), p. 756.
27. R.R. Gould and M.J. Waldren, op. cit.
28. Ibid.
29. *Daily Mail* (17 May 1994).
30. Ibid.
31. *The Relay* (March 1994).
32. *Police* (June 1994), p. 21.
33. R.W. Gould and M.J. Waldren, op. cit.

34. *Daily Telegraph* (29 Dec. 1972).
35. *Daily Mail* (9 Dec. 1975).
36. *Daily Telegraph* (13 Dec. 1975).
37. M. Shersby, 'Why we don't want arms', *Police* (Dec. 1993).
38. Anon., 'Cannon fodder in the line of fire', *Police* (June 1994), p. 20.
39. *Policing Today* (Oct. 1994), p. 50.
40. M. Shersby, op. cit.
41. Anon., *Killed in the Line of Duty* (Washington DC: Department of Justice, 1992).
42. M. Shersby, op. cit.
43. Anon., 'Armed seige tactics defended', *Police Review*.
44. R. Reiner, *The Politics of the Police* (Hemel Hempstead: Harvester, 1985).
45. I. McKenzie, 'Trigger Happy', *Police Review* (10 Jan. 1992), p. 68.
46. I. McKenzie, ibid, p. 68.
47. M. Shersby, op. cit.
48. US Department of Justice, op. cit.
49. Royal Commission on Capital Punishment (1953), Cmd. 8932, p. 27.
50. Chester Stern, 'More guns for the Deadly Force', *Mail on Sunday* (22 Oct. 1995).

Further reading and selected bibliography

Anon, *Killed in the Line of Duty* (Washington DC: Department of Justice, 1992).

Butcher, B.D., *A Moving Rambling Police* (Norwich: Norfolk Constabulary, 1989).

Dobson, B., *Policing in Lancashire 1839–1989* (Blackpool: Landy Publishing, 1989).

Emsley, C., *Crime and Society in England 1750–1900* (London: Longman, 1987).

Emsley, C., *The English Police* (Hemel Hempstead: Harvester Wheatsheaf, 1991).

Gould, R.W. and Waldren, M.J., *London's Armed Police* (London: Arms & Armour Press, 1986).

Ingleton, R., *The Gentlemen at War: Policing Britain 1939–45* (Maidstone: Cranborne Publications, 1994).

McRae, H., *The World in 2020* (London: Harper/Collins, 1994).

Reiner, R., *The Politics of the Police* (Hemel Hempstead: Harvester, 1985).

White, J., *The Worst Street in North London* (London: Routledge & Kegan Paul, 1986).

Index